CAREER EXAMINATION SERIES

THIS IS YOUR **PASSBOOK**® FOR ...

PUBLIC INFORMATION SPECIALIST

NLC®

NATIONAL LEARNING CORPORATION®
passbooks.com

COPYRIGHT NOTICE

Copyright © 2022 by

NLC®

National Learning Corporation

212 Michael Drive, Syosset, NY 11791
(516) 921-8888 • www.passbooks.com
E-mail: info@passbooks.com

PUBLISHED IN THE UNITED STATES OF AMERICA

PASSBOOK® SERIES

THE *PASSBOOK® SERIES* has been created to prepare applicants and candidates for the ultimate academic battlefield – the examination room.

At some time in our lives, each and every one of us may be required to take an examination – for validation, matriculation, admission, qualification, registration, certification, or licensure.

Based on the assumption that every applicant or candidate has met the basic formal educational standards, has taken the required number of courses, and read the necessary texts, the *PASSBOOK® SERIES* furnishes the one special preparation which may assure passing with confidence, instead of failing with insecurity. Examination questions – together with answers – are furnished as the basic vehicle for study so that the mysteries of the examination and its compounding difficulties may be eliminated or diminished by a sure method.

This book is meant to help you pass your examination provided that you qualify and are serious in your objective.

The entire field is reviewed through the huge store of content information which is succinctly presented through a provocative and challenging approach – the question-and-answer method.

A climate of success is established by furnishing the correct answers at the end of each test.

You soon learn to recognize types of questions, forms of questions, and patterns of questioning. You may even begin to anticipate expected outcomes.

You perceive that many questions are repeated or adapted so that you can gain acute insights, which may enable you to score many sure points.

You learn how to confront new questions, or types of questions, and to attack them confidently and work out the correct answers.

You note objectives and emphases, and recognize pitfalls and dangers, so that you may make positive educational adjustments.

Moreover, you are kept fully informed in relation to new concepts, methods, practices, and directions in the field.

You discover that you arre actually taking the examination all the time: you are preparing for the examination by "taking" an examination, not by reading extraneous and/or supererogatory textbooks.

In short, this PASSBOOK®, used directedly, should be an important factor in helping you to pass your test.

PUBLIC INFORMATION SPECIALIST

DUTIES:

As a **Public Information Specialist I**, you would work independently and perform the full range of public information activities for your agency. Such activities may include acting as spokesperson for an agency to the news media and to individuals who inquire regarding the agency's activities. You may draft, edit and distribute informational material concerning your agency's activities. You may conduct tours, prepare speeches and presentations, oversee your agency's website content and social media channels to develop and execute digital campaigns to promote your agency's public information objectives. You may supervise lower level employees including support, creative, and information technology staff.

As a **Public Information Specialist II**, you would direct and evaluate a public information program or a major segment of a large program and consult with management both verbally and in writing on means of improving public information program effectiveness within your agency. You would perform all the duties of a Public Information Specialist I. You may supervise lower level employees including support, creative and information technology staff by establishing work and production schedules, training and evaluating staff's performance and suggesting and initiating changes or new techniques in the agency's public information objectives to improve your agency's overall public information effectiveness.

SUBJECT OF EXAMINATION:

The written test is designed to test for knowledge, skills, and/or abilities in such areas as:

1. **Educating and interacting with the public** - These questions test for the ability to communicate with others in a manner consistent with good public relations practices. Questions will cover such concepts as interviewing or gathering information from others; participating in meetings or work groups; and presenting information to citizens, community organizations, staff and the media.

2. **Preparing public information materials** - These questions test for the ability to prepare basic informational materials electronically and in print, for the public and the media, including such products as correspondence, brochures, and news releases. Questions may cover such topics as selecting content to effectively communicate with the intended audience, making decisions regarding page readability of text, and using graphics, photographs, headlines, or captions to enhance a message.

3. **Preparing written material** - These questions test for the ability to present information clearly and accurately, and to organize paragraphs logically and comprehensibly. For some questions, you will be given information in two or three sentences followed by four restatements of the information. You must then choose the best version. For other questions, you will be given paragraphs with their sentences out of order. You must then choose, from four suggestions, the best order for the sentences.

4. **Grammar, usage, punctuation, and editing** - These questions test for the ability to generate, prepare, and edit written documents. Some questions test for a knowledge of grammar, usage, punctuation, and sentence structure. Others test for the ability to edit sentences to produce correct, clear, concise copy.

5. **Directing a public information program** - These questions test for the ability to conduct a public information program for a department or agency. Questions may cover such topics as evaluating needs, planning publicity programs, developing relations with the community and media, and directing the activities of a public relations or marketing plan.

HOW TO TAKE A TEST

I. YOU MUST PASS AN EXAMINATION

A. *WHAT EVERY CANDIDATE SHOULD KNOW*

Examination applicants often ask us for help in preparing for the written test. What can I study in advance? What kinds of questions will be asked? How will the test be given? How will the papers be graded?

As an applicant for a civil service examination, you may be wondering about some of these things. Our purpose here is to suggest effective methods of advance study and to describe civil service examinations.

Your chances for success on this examination can be increased if you know how to prepare. Those "pre-examination jitters" can be reduced if you know what to expect. You can even experience an adventure in good citizenship if you know why civil service exams are given.

B. *WHY ARE CIVIL SERVICE EXAMINATIONS GIVEN?*

Civil service examinations are important to you in two ways. As a citizen, you want public jobs filled by employees who know how to do their work. As a job seeker, you want a fair chance to compete for that job on an equal footing with other candidates. The best-known means of accomplishing this two-fold goal is the competitive examination.

Exams are widely publicized throughout the nation. They may be administered for jobs in federal, state, city, municipal, town or village governments or agencies.

Any citizen may apply, with some limitations, such as the age or residence of applicants. Your experience and education may be reviewed to see whether you meet the requirements for the particular examination. When these requirements exist, they are reasonable and applied consistently to all applicants. Thus, a competitive examination may cause you some uneasiness now, but it is your privilege and safeguard.

C. *HOW ARE CIVIL SERVICE EXAMS DEVELOPED?*

Examinations are carefully written by trained technicians who are specialists in the field known as "psychological measurement," in consultation with recognized authorities in the field of work that the test will cover. These experts recommend the subject matter areas or skills to be tested; only those knowledges or skills important to your success on the job are included. The most reliable books and source materials available are used as references. Together, the experts and technicians judge the difficulty level of the questions.

Test technicians know how to phrase questions so that the problem is clearly stated. Their ethics do not permit "trick" or "catch" questions. Questions may have been tried out on sample groups, or subjected to statistical analysis, to determine their usefulness.

Written tests are often used in combination with performance tests, ratings of training and experience, and oral interviews. All of these measures combine to form the best-known means of finding the right person for the right job.

II. HOW TO PASS THE WRITTEN TEST

A. NATURE OF THE EXAMINATION

To prepare intelligently for civil service examinations, you should know how they differ from school examinations you have taken. In school you were assigned certain definite pages to read or subjects to cover. The examination questions were quite detailed and usually emphasized memory. Civil service exams, on the other hand, try to discover your present ability to perform the duties of a position, plus your potentiality to learn these duties. In other words, a civil service exam attempts to predict how successful you will be. Questions cover such a broad area that they cannot be as minute and detailed as school exam questions.

In the public service similar kinds of work, or positions, are grouped together in one "class." This process is known as *position-classification*. All the positions in a class are paid according to the salary range for that class. One class title covers all of these positions, and they are all tested by the same examination.

B. FOUR BASIC STEPS

1) Study the announcement

How, then, can you know what subjects to study? Our best answer is: "Learn as much as possible about the class of positions for which you've applied." The exam will test the knowledge, skills and abilities needed to do the work.

Your most valuable source of information about the position you want is the official exam announcement. This announcement lists the training and experience qualifications. Check these standards and apply only if you come reasonably close to meeting them.

The brief description of the position in the examination announcement offers some clues to the subjects which will be tested. Think about the job itself. Review the duties in your mind. Can you perform them, or are there some in which you are rusty? Fill in the blank spots in your preparation.

Many jurisdictions preview the written test in the exam announcement by including a section called "Knowledge and Abilities Required," "Scope of the Examination," or some similar heading. Here you will find out specifically what fields will be tested.

2) Review your own background

Once you learn in general what the position is all about, and what you need to know to do the work, ask yourself which subjects you already know fairly well and which need improvement. You may wonder whether to concentrate on improving your strong areas or on building some background in your fields of weakness. When the announcement has specified "some knowledge" or "considerable knowledge," or has used adjectives like "beginning principles of…" or "advanced … methods," you can get a clue as to the number and difficulty of questions to be asked in any given field. More questions, and hence broader coverage, would be included for those subjects which are more important in the work. Now weigh your strengths and weaknesses against the job requirements and prepare accordingly.

3) Determine the level of the position

Another way to tell how intensively you should prepare is to understand the level of the job for which you are applying. Is it the entering level? In other words, is this the position in which beginners in a field of work are hired? Or is it an intermediate or advanced level? Sometimes this is indicated by such words as "Junior" or "Senior" in the class title. Other jurisdictions use Roman numerals to designate the level – Clerk I, Clerk II, for example. The word "Supervisor" sometimes appears in the title. If the level is not indicated by the title, check the description of duties. Will you be working under very close supervision, or will you have responsibility for independent decisions in this work?

4) Choose appropriate study materials

Now that you know the subjects to be examined and the relative amount of each subject to be covered, you can choose suitable study materials. For beginning level jobs, or even advanced ones, if you have a pronounced weakness in some aspect of your training, read a modern, standard textbook in that field. Be sure it is up to date and has general coverage. Such books are normally available at your library, and the librarian will be glad to help you locate one. For entry-level positions, questions of appropriate difficulty are chosen – neither highly advanced questions, nor those too simple. Such questions require careful thought but not advanced training.

If the position for which you are applying is technical or advanced, you will read more advanced, specialized material. If you are already familiar with the basic principles of your field, elementary textbooks would waste your time. Concentrate on advanced textbooks and technical periodicals. Think through the concepts and review difficult problems in your field.

These are all general sources. You can get more ideas on your own initiative, following these leads. For example, training manuals and publications of the government agency which employs workers in your field can be useful, particularly for technical and professional positions. A letter or visit to the government department involved may result in more specific study suggestions, and certainly will provide you with a more definite idea of the exact nature of the position you are seeking.

III. KINDS OF TESTS

Tests are used for purposes other than measuring knowledge and ability to perform specified duties. For some positions, it is equally important to test ability to make adjustments to new situations or to profit from training. In others, basic mental abilities not dependent on information are essential. Questions which test these things may not appear as pertinent to the duties of the position as those which test for knowledge and information. Yet they are often highly important parts of a fair examination. For very general questions, it is almost impossible to help you direct your study efforts. What we can do is to point out some of the more common of these general abilities needed in public service positions and describe some typical questions.

1) General information

Broad, general information has been found useful for predicting job success in some kinds of work. This is tested in a variety of ways, from vocabulary lists to questions about current events. Basic background in some field of work, such as sociology or economics, may be sampled in a group of questions. Often these are principles which have become familiar to most persons through exposure rather than through formal training. It is difficult to advise you how to study for these questions; being alert to the world around you is our best suggestion.

2) Verbal ability

An example of an ability needed in many positions is verbal or language ability. Verbal ability is, in brief, the ability to use and understand words. Vocabulary and grammar tests are typical measures of this ability. Reading comprehension or paragraph interpretation questions are common in many kinds of civil service tests. You are given a paragraph of written material and asked to find its central meaning.

3) Numerical ability

Number skills can be tested by the familiar arithmetic problem, by checking paired lists of numbers to see which are alike and which are different, or by interpreting charts and graphs. In the latter test, a graph may be printed in the test booklet which you are asked to use as the basis for answering questions.

4) Observation

A popular test for law-enforcement positions is the observation test. A picture is shown to you for several minutes, then taken away. Questions about the picture test your ability to observe both details and larger elements.

5) Following directions

In many positions in the public service, the employee must be able to carry out written instructions dependably and accurately. You may be given a chart with several columns, each column listing a variety of information. The questions require you to carry out directions involving the information given in the chart.

6) Skills and aptitudes

Performance tests effectively measure some manual skills and aptitudes. When the skill is one in which you are trained, such as typing or shorthand, you can practice. These tests are often very much like those given in business school or high school courses. For many of the other skills and aptitudes, however, no short-time preparation can be made. Skills and abilities natural to you or that you have developed throughout your lifetime are being tested.

Many of the general questions just described provide all the data needed to answer the questions and ask you to use your reasoning ability to find the answers. Your best preparation for these tests, as well as for tests of facts and ideas, is to be at your physical and mental best. You, no doubt, have your own methods of getting into an exam-taking mood and keeping "in shape." The next section lists some ideas on this subject.

IV. KINDS OF QUESTIONS

Only rarely is the "essay" question, which you answer in narrative form, used in civil service tests. Civil service tests are usually of the short-answer type. Full instructions for answering these questions will be given to you at the examination. But in case this is your first experience with short-answer questions and separate answer sheets, here is what you need to know:

1) Multiple-choice Questions

Most popular of the short-answer questions is the "multiple choice" or "best answer" question. It can be used, for example, to test for factual knowledge, ability to solve problems or judgment in meeting situations found at work.

A multiple-choice question is normally one of three types—

- It can begin with an incomplete statement followed by several possible endings. You are to find the one ending which *best* completes the statement, although some of the others may not be entirely wrong.
- It can also be a complete statement in the form of a question which is answered by choosing one of the statements listed.
- It can be in the form of a problem – again you select the best answer.

Here is an example of a multiple-choice question with a discussion which should give you some clues as to the method for choosing the right answer:

When an employee has a complaint about his assignment, the action which will *best* help him overcome his difficulty is to
  A. discuss his difficulty with his coworkers
  B. take the problem to the head of the organization
  C. take the problem to the person who gave him the assignment
  D. say nothing to anyone about his complaint

In answering this question, you should study each of the choices to find which is best. Consider choice "A" – Certainly an employee may discuss his complaint with fellow employees, but no change or improvement can result, and the complaint remains unresolved. Choice "B" is a poor choice since the head of the organization probably does not know what assignment you have been given, and taking your problem to him is known as "going over the head" of the supervisor. The supervisor, or person who made the assignment, is the person who can clarify it or correct any injustice. Choice "C" is, therefore, correct. To say nothing, as in choice "D," is unwise. Supervisors have and interest in knowing the problems employees are facing, and the employee is seeking a solution to his problem.

2) True/False Questions

The "true/false" or "right/wrong" form of question is sometimes used. Here a complete statement is given. Your job is to decide whether the statement is right or wrong.

SAMPLE: A roaming cell-phone call to a nearby city costs less than a non-roaming call to a distant city.

This statement is wrong, or false, since roaming calls are more expensive.
This is not a complete list of all possible question forms, although most of the others are variations of these common types. You will always get complete directions for

answering questions. Be sure you understand *how* to mark your answers – ask questions until you do.

V. RECORDING YOUR ANSWERS

Computer terminals are used more and more today for many different kinds of exams.

For an examination with very few applicants, you may be told to record your answers in the test booklet itself. Separate answer sheets are much more common. If this separate answer sheet is to be scored by machine – and this is often the case – it is highly important that you mark your answers correctly in order to get credit.

An electronic scoring machine is often used in civil service offices because of the speed with which papers can be scored. Machine-scored answer sheets must be marked with a pencil, which will be given to you. This pencil has a high graphite content which responds to the electronic scoring machine. As a matter of fact, stray dots may register as answers, so do not let your pencil rest on the answer sheet while you are pondering the correct answer. Also, if your pencil lead breaks or is otherwise defective, ask for another.

Since the answer sheet will be dropped in a slot in the scoring machine, be careful not to bend the corners or get the paper crumpled.

The answer sheet normally has five vertical columns of numbers, with 30 numbers to a column. These numbers correspond to the question numbers in your test booklet. After each number, going across the page are four or five pairs of dotted lines. These short dotted lines have small letters or numbers above them. The first two pairs may also have a "T" or "F" above the letters. This indicates that the first two pairs only are to be used if the questions are of the true-false type. If the questions are multiple choice, disregard the "T" and "F" and pay attention only to the small letters or numbers.

Answer your questions in the manner of the sample that follows:

32. The largest city in the United States is
    A. Washington, D.C.
    B. New York City
    C. Chicago
    D. Detroit
    E. San Francisco

1) Choose the answer you think is best. (New York City is the largest, so "B" is correct.)
2) Find the row of dotted lines numbered the same as the question you are answering. (Find row number 32)
3) Find the pair of dotted lines corresponding to the answer. (Find the pair of lines under the mark "B.")
4) Make a solid black mark between the dotted lines.

VI. BEFORE THE TEST

Common sense will help you find procedures to follow to get ready for an examination. Too many of us, however, overlook these sensible measures. Indeed, nervousness and fatigue have been found to be the most serious reasons why applicants fail to do their best on civil service tests. Here is a list of reminders:

- Begin your preparation early – Don't wait until the last minute to go scurrying around for books and materials or to find out what the position is all about.
- Prepare continuously – An hour a night for a week is better than an all-night cram session. This has been definitely established. What is more, a night a week for a month will return better dividends than crowding your study into a shorter period of time.
- Locate the place of the exam – You have been sent a notice telling you when and where to report for the examination. If the location is in a different town or otherwise unfamiliar to you, it would be well to inquire the best route and learn something about the building.
- Relax the night before the test – Allow your mind to rest. Do not study at all that night. Plan some mild recreation or diversion; then go to bed early and get a good night's sleep.
- Get up early enough to make a leisurely trip to the place for the test – This way unforeseen events, traffic snarls, unfamiliar buildings, etc. will not upset you.
- Dress comfortably – A written test is not a fashion show. You will be known by number and not by name, so wear something comfortable.
- Leave excess paraphernalia at home – Shopping bags and odd bundles will get in your way. You need bring only the items mentioned in the official notice you received; usually everything you need is provided. Do not bring reference books to the exam. They will only confuse those last minutes and be taken away from you when in the test room.
- Arrive somewhat ahead of time – If because of transportation schedules you must get there very early, bring a newspaper or magazine to take your mind off yourself while waiting.
- Locate the examination room – When you have found the proper room, you will be directed to the seat or part of the room where you will sit. Sometimes you are given a sheet of instructions to read while you are waiting. Do not fill out any forms until you are told to do so; just read them and be prepared.
- Relax and prepare to listen to the instructions
- If you have any physical problem that may keep you from doing your best, be sure to tell the test administrator. If you are sick or in poor health, you really cannot do your best on the exam. You can come back and take the test some other time.

VII. AT THE TEST

The day of the test is here and you have the test booklet in your hand. The temptation to get going is very strong. Caution! There is more to success than knowing the right answers. You must know how to identify your papers and understand variations in the type of short-answer question used in this particular examination. Follow these suggestions for maximum results from your efforts:

1) Cooperate with the monitor

The test administrator has a duty to create a situation in which you can be as much at ease as possible. He will give instructions, tell you when to begin, check to see that you are marking your answer sheet correctly, and so on. He is not there to guard you, although he will see that your competitors do not take unfair advantage. He wants to help you do your best.

2) Listen to all instructions

Don't jump the gun! Wait until you understand all directions. In most civil service tests you get more time than you need to answer the questions. So don't be in a hurry. Read each word of instructions until you clearly understand the meaning. Study the examples, listen to all announcements and follow directions. Ask questions if you do not understand what to do.

3) Identify your papers

Civil service exams are usually identified by number only. You will be assigned a number; you must not put your name on your test papers. Be sure to copy your number correctly. Since more than one exam may be given, copy your exact examination title.

4) Plan your time

Unless you are told that a test is a "speed" or "rate of work" test, speed itself is usually not important. Time enough to answer all the questions will be provided, but this does not mean that you have all day. An overall time limit has been set. Divide the total time (in minutes) by the number of questions to determine the approximate time you have for each question.

5) Do not linger over difficult questions

If you come across a difficult question, mark it with a paper clip (useful to have along) and come back to it when you have been through the booklet. One caution if you do this – be sure to skip a number on your answer sheet as well. Check often to be sure that you have not lost your place and that you are marking in the row numbered the same as the question you are answering.

6) Read the questions

Be sure you know what the question asks! Many capable people are unsuccessful because they failed to *read* the questions correctly.

7) Answer all questions

Unless you have been instructed that a penalty will be deducted for incorrect answers, it is better to guess than to omit a question.

8) Speed tests

It is often better NOT to guess on speed tests. It has been found that on timed tests people are tempted to spend the last few seconds before time is called in marking answers at random – without even reading them – in the hope of picking up a few extra points. To discourage this practice, the instructions may warn you that your score will be "corrected" for guessing. That is, a penalty will be applied. The incorrect answers will be deducted from the correct ones, or some other penalty formula will be used.

9

9) Review your answers

If you finish before time is called, go back to the questions you guessed or omitted to give them further thought. Review other answers if you have time.

10) Return your test materials

If you are ready to leave before others have finished or time is called, take ALL your materials to the monitor and leave quietly. Never take any test material with you. The monitor can discover whose papers are not complete, and taking a test booklet may be grounds for disqualification.

VIII. EXAMINATION TECHNIQUES

1) Read the general instructions carefully. These are usually printed on the first page of the exam booklet. As a rule, these instructions refer to the timing of the examination; the fact that you should not start work until the signal and must stop work at a signal, etc. If there are any *special* instructions, such as a choice of questions to be answered, make sure that you note this instruction carefully.

2) When you are ready to start work on the examination, that is as soon as the signal has been given, read the instructions to each question booklet, underline any key words or phrases, such as *least*, *best*, *outline*, *describe* and the like. In this way you will tend to answer as requested rather than discover on reviewing your paper that you *listed without describing*, that you selected the *worst* choice rather than the *best* choice, etc.

3) If the examination is of the objective or multiple-choice type – that is, each question will also give a series of possible answers: A, B, C or D, and you are called upon to select the best answer and write the letter next to that answer on your answer paper – it is advisable to start answering each question in turn. There may be anywhere from 50 to 100 such questions in the three or four hours allotted and you can see how much time would be taken if you read through all the questions before beginning to answer any. Furthermore, if you come across a question or group of questions which you know would be difficult to answer, it would undoubtedly affect your handling of all the other questions.

4) If the examination is of the essay type and contains but a few questions, it is a moot point as to whether you should read all the questions before starting to answer any one. Of course, if you are given a choice – say five out of seven and the like – then it is essential to read all the questions so you can eliminate the two that are most difficult. If, however, you are asked to answer all the questions, there may be danger in trying to answer the easiest one first because you may find that you will spend too much time on it. The best technique is to answer the first question, then proceed to the second, etc.

5) Time your answers. Before the exam begins, write down the time it started, then add the time allowed for the examination and write down the time it must be completed, then divide the time available somewhat as follows:

- If 3-1/2 hours are allowed, that would be 210 minutes. If you have 80 objective-type questions, that would be an average of 2-1/2 minutes per question. Allow yourself no more than 2 minutes per question, or a total of 160 minutes, which will permit about 50 minutes to review.
- If for the time allotment of 210 minutes there are 7 essay questions to answer, that would average about 30 minutes a question. Give yourself only 25 minutes per question so that you have about 35 minutes to review.

6) The most important instruction is to *read each question* and make sure you know what is wanted. The second most important instruction is to *time yourself properly* so that you answer every question. The third most important instruction is to *answer every question*. Guess if you have to but include something for each question. Remember that you will receive no credit for a blank and will probably receive some credit if you write something in answer to an essay question. If you guess a letter – say "B" for a multiple-choice question – you may have guessed right. If you leave a blank as an answer to a multiple-choice question, the examiners may respect your feelings but it will not add a point to your score. Some exams may penalize you for wrong answers, so in such cases *only*, you may not want to guess unless you have some basis for your answer.

7) Suggestions
   a. Objective-type questions
      1. Examine the question booklet for proper sequence of pages and questions
      2. Read all instructions carefully
      3. Skip any question which seems too difficult; return to it after all other questions have been answered
      4. Apportion your time properly; do not spend too much time on any single question or group of questions
      5. Note and underline key words – *all, most, fewest, least, best, worst, same, opposite,* etc.
      6. Pay particular attention to negatives
      7. Note unusual option, e.g., unduly long, short, complex, different or similar in content to the body of the question
      8. Observe the use of "hedging" words – *probably, may, most likely,* etc.
      9. Make sure that your answer is put next to the same number as the question
      10. Do not second-guess unless you have good reason to believe the second answer is definitely more correct
      11. Cross out original answer if you decide another answer is more accurate; do not erase until you are ready to hand your paper in
      12. Answer all questions; guess unless instructed otherwise
      13. Leave time for review

   b. Essay questions
      1. Read each question carefully
      2. Determine exactly what is wanted. Underline key words or phrases.
      3. Decide on outline or paragraph answer

4. Include many different points and elements unless asked to develop any one or two points or elements
5. Show impartiality by giving pros and cons unless directed to select one side only
6. Make and write down any assumptions you find necessary to answer the questions
7. Watch your English, grammar, punctuation and choice of words
8. Time your answers; don't crowd material

8) Answering the essay question

Most essay questions can be answered by framing the specific response around several key words or ideas. Here are a few such key words or ideas:

M's: manpower, materials, methods, money, management
P's: purpose, program, policy, plan, procedure, practice, problems, pitfalls, personnel, public relations

a. Six basic steps in handling problems:
   1. Preliminary plan and background development
   2. Collect information, data and facts
   3. Analyze and interpret information, data and facts
   4. Analyze and develop solutions as well as make recommendations
   5. Prepare report and sell recommendations
   6. Install recommendations and follow up effectiveness

b. Pitfalls to avoid
   1. *Taking things for granted* – A statement of the situation does not necessarily imply that each of the elements is necessarily true; for example, a complaint may be invalid and biased so that all that can be taken for granted is that a complaint has been registered
   2. *Considering only one side of a situation* – Wherever possible, indicate several alternatives and then point out the reasons you selected the best one
   3. *Failing to indicate follow up* – Whenever your answer indicates action on your part, make certain that you will take proper follow-up action to see how successful your recommendations, procedures or actions turn out to be
   4. *Taking too long in answering any single question* – Remember to time your answers properly

IX. AFTER THE TEST

Scoring procedures differ in detail among civil service jurisdictions although the general principles are the same. Whether the papers are hand-scored or graded by machine we have described, they are nearly always graded by number. That is, the person who marks the paper knows only the number – never the name – of the applicant. Not until all the papers have been graded will they be matched with names. If other tests, such as training and experience or oral interview ratings have been given, scores will be combined. Different parts of the examination usually have different weights. For example, the written test might count 60 percent of the final grade, and a rating of training and experience 40 percent. In many jurisdictions, veterans will have a certain number of points added to their grades.

After the final grade has been determined, the names are placed in grade order and an eligible list is established. There are various methods for resolving ties between those who get the same final grade – probably the most common is to place first the name of the person whose application was received first. Job offers are made from the eligible list in the order the names appear on it. You will be notified of your grade and your rank as soon as all these computations have been made. This will be done as rapidly as possible.

People who are found to meet the requirements in the announcement are called "eligibles." Their names are put on a list of eligible candidates. An eligible's chances of getting a job depend on how high he stands on this list and how fast agencies are filling jobs from the list.

When a job is to be filled from a list of eligibles, the agency asks for the names of people on the list of eligibles for that job. When the civil service commission receives this request, it sends to the agency the names of the three people highest on this list. Or, if the job to be filled has specialized requirements, the office sends the agency the names of the top three persons who meet these requirements from the general list.

The appointing officer makes a choice from among the three people whose names were sent to him. If the selected person accepts the appointment, the names of the others are put back on the list to be considered for future openings.

That is the rule in hiring from all kinds of eligible lists, whether they are for typist, carpenter, chemist, or something else. For every vacancy, the appointing officer has his choice of any one of the top three eligibles on the list. This explains why the person whose name is on top of the list sometimes does not get an appointment when some of the persons lower on the list do. If the appointing officer chooses the second or third eligible, the No. 1 eligible does not get a job at once, but stays on the list until he is appointed or the list is terminated.

X. HOW TO PASS THE INTERVIEW TEST

The examination for which you applied requires an oral interview test. You have already taken the written test and you are now being called for the interview test – the final part of the formal examination.

You may think that it is not possible to prepare for an interview test and that there are no procedures to follow during an interview. Our purpose is to point out some things you can do in advance that will help you and some good rules to follow and pitfalls to avoid while you are being interviewed.

What is an interview supposed to test?

The written examination is designed to test the technical knowledge and competence of the candidate; the oral is designed to evaluate intangible qualities, not readily measured otherwise, and to establish a list showing the relative fitness of each candidate – as measured against his competitors – for the position sought. Scoring is not on the basis of "right" and "wrong," but on a sliding scale of values ranging from "not passable" to "outstanding." As a matter of fact, it is possible to achieve a relatively low score without a single "incorrect" answer because of evident weakness in the qualities being measured.

Occasionally, an examination may consist entirely of an oral test – either an individual or a group oral. In such cases, information is sought concerning the technical knowledges and abilities of the candidate, since there has been no written examination for this purpose. More commonly, however, an oral test is used to supplement a written examination.

Who conducts interviews?

The composition of oral boards varies among different jurisdictions. In nearly all, a representative of the personnel department serves as chairman. One of the members of the board may be a representative of the department in which the candidate would work. In some cases, "outside experts" are used, and, frequently, a businessman or some other representative of the general public is asked to serve. Labor and management or other special groups may be represented. The aim is to secure the services of experts in the appropriate field.

However the board is composed, it is a good idea (and not at all improper or unethical) to ascertain in advance of the interview who the members are and what groups they represent. When you are introduced to them, you will have some idea of their backgrounds and interests, and at least you will not stutter and stammer over their names.

What should be done before the interview?

While knowledge about the board members is useful and takes some of the surprise element out of the interview, there is other preparation which is more substantive. It *is* possible to prepare for an oral interview – in several ways:

1) Keep a copy of your application and review it carefully before the interview

This may be the only document before the oral board, and the starting point of the interview. Know what education and experience you have listed there, and the sequence and dates of all of it. Sometimes the board will ask you to review the highlights of your experience for them; you should not have to hem and haw doing it.

2) Study the class specification and the examination announcement

Usually, the oral board has one or both of these to guide them. The qualities, characteristics or knowledges required by the position sought are stated in these documents. They offer valuable clues as to the nature of the oral interview. For example, if the job involves supervisory responsibilities, the announcement will usually indicate that knowledge of modern supervisory methods and the qualifications of the candidate as a supervisor will be tested. If so, you can expect such questions, frequently in the form of a hypothetical situation which you are expected to solve. NEVER go into an oral without knowledge of the duties and responsibilities of the job you seek.

3) Think through each qualification required

Try to visualize the kind of questions you would ask if you were a board member. How well could you answer them? Try especially to appraise your own knowledge and background in each area, *measured against the job sought*, and identify any areas in which you are weak. Be critical and realistic – do not flatter yourself.

4) Do some general reading in areas in which you feel you may be weak

For example, if the job involves supervision and your past experience has NOT, some general reading in supervisory methods and practices, particularly in the field of human relations, might be useful. Do NOT study agency procedures or detailed manuals. The oral board will be testing your understanding and capacity, not your memory.

5) Get a good night's sleep and watch your general health and mental attitude

You will want a clear head at the interview. Take care of a cold or any other minor ailment, and of course, no hangovers.

What should be done on the day of the interview?

Now comes the day of the interview itself. Give yourself plenty of time to get there. Plan to arrive somewhat ahead of the scheduled time, particularly if your appointment is in the fore part of the day. If a previous candidate fails to appear, the board might be ready for you a bit early. By early afternoon an oral board is almost invariably behind schedule if there are many candidates, and you may have to wait. Take along a book or magazine to read, or your application to review, but leave any extraneous material in the waiting room when you go in for your interview. In any event, relax and compose yourself.

The matter of dress is important. The board is forming impressions about you – from your experience, your manners, your attitude, and your appearance. Give your personal appearance careful attention. Dress your best, but not your flashiest. Choose conservative, appropriate clothing, and be sure it is immaculate. This is a business interview, and your appearance should indicate that you regard it as such. Besides, being well groomed and properly dressed will help boost your confidence.

Sooner or later, someone will call your name and escort you into the interview room. *This is it.* From here on you are on your own. It is too late for any more preparation. But remember, you asked for this opportunity to prove your fitness, and you are here because your request was granted.

What happens when you go in?

The usual sequence of events will be as follows: The clerk (who is often the board stenographer) will introduce you to the chairman of the oral board, who will introduce you to the other members of the board. Acknowledge the introductions before you sit down. Do not be surprised if you find a microphone facing you or a stenotypist sitting by. Oral interviews are usually recorded in the event of an appeal or other review.

Usually the chairman of the board will open the interview by reviewing the highlights of your education and work experience from your application – primarily for the benefit of the other members of the board, as well as to get the material into the record. Do not interrupt or comment unless there is an error or significant misinterpretation; if that is the case, do not hesitate. But do not quibble about insignificant matters. Also, he will usually ask you some question about your education, experience or your present job – partly to get you to start talking and to establish the interviewing "rapport." He may start the actual questioning, or turn it over to one of the other members. Frequently, each member undertakes the questioning on a particular area, one in which he is perhaps most competent, so you can expect each member to participate in the examination. Because time is limited, you may also expect some rather abrupt switches in the direction the questioning takes, so do not be upset by it. Normally, a board member will not pursue a single line of questioning unless he discovers a particular strength or weakness.

After each member has participated, the chairman will usually ask whether any member has any further questions, then will ask you if you have anything you wish to add. Unless you are expecting this question, it may floor you. Worse, it may start you off on an extended, extemporaneous speech. The board is not usually seeking more information. The question is principally to offer you a last opportunity to present further qualifications or to indicate that you have nothing to add. So, if you feel that a significant qualification or characteristic has been overlooked, it is proper to point it out in a sentence or so. Do not compliment the board on the thoroughness of their examination – they have been sketchy, and you know it. If you wish, merely say, "No thank you, I have nothing further to add." This is a point where you can "talk yourself out" of a good impression or fail to present an important bit of information. Remember, *you close the interview yourself.*

The chairman will then say, "That is all, Mr. _____, thank you." Do not be startled; the interview is over, and quicker than you think. Thank him, gather your belongings and take your leave. Save your sigh of relief for the other side of the door.

How to put your best foot forward

Throughout this entire process, you may feel that the board individually and collectively is trying to pierce your defenses, seek out your hidden weaknesses and embarrass and confuse you. Actually, this is not true. They are obliged to make an appraisal of your qualifications for the job you are seeking, and they want to see you in your best light. Remember, they must interview all candidates and a non-cooperative candidate may become a failure in spite of their best efforts to bring out his qualifications. Here are 15 suggestions that will help you:

1) Be natural – Keep your attitude confident, not cocky

If you are not confident that you can do the job, do not expect the board to be. Do not apologize for your weaknesses, try to bring out your strong points. The board is interested in a positive, not negative, presentation. Cockiness will antagonize any board member and make him wonder if you are covering up a weakness by a false show of strength.

2) Get comfortable, but don't lounge or sprawl

Sit erectly but not stiffly. A careless posture may lead the board to conclude that you are careless in other things, or at least that you are not impressed by the importance of the occasion. Either conclusion is natural, even if incorrect. Do not fuss with your clothing, a pencil or an ashtray. Your hands may occasionally be useful to emphasize a point; do not let them become a point of distraction.

3) Do not wisecrack or make small talk

This is a serious situation, and your attitude should show that you consider it as such. Further, the time of the board is limited – they do not want to waste it, and neither should you.

4) Do not exaggerate your experience or abilities

In the first place, from information in the application or other interviews and sources, the board may know more about you than you think. Secondly, you probably will not get away with it. An experienced board is rather adept at spotting such a situation, so do not take the chance.

5) If you know a board member, do not make a point of it, yet do not hide it

Certainly you are not fooling him, and probably not the other members of the board. Do not try to take advantage of your acquaintanceship – it will probably do you little good.

6) Do not dominate the interview

Let the board do that. They will give you the clues – do not assume that you have to do all the talking. Realize that the board has a number of questions to ask you, and do not try to take up all the interview time by showing off your extensive knowledge of the answer to the first one.

7) Be attentive

You only have 20 minutes or so, and you should keep your attention at its sharpest throughout. When a member is addressing a problem or question to you, give him your undivided attention. Address your reply principally to him, but do not exclude the other board members.

8) Do not interrupt

A board member may be stating a problem for you to analyze. He will ask you a question when the time comes. Let him state the problem, and wait for the question.

9) Make sure you understand the question

Do not try to answer until you are sure what the question is. If it is not clear, restate it in your own words or ask the board member to clarify it for you. However, do not haggle about minor elements.

10) Reply promptly but not hastily

A common entry on oral board rating sheets is "candidate responded readily," or "candidate hesitated in replies." Respond as promptly and quickly as you can, but do not jump to a hasty, ill-considered answer.

11) Do not be peremptory in your answers

A brief answer is proper – but do not fire your answer back. That is a losing game from your point of view. The board member can probably ask questions much faster than you can answer them.

12) Do not try to create the answer you think the board member wants

He is interested in what kind of mind you have and how it works – not in playing games. Furthermore, he can usually spot this practice and will actually grade you down on it.

13) Do not switch sides in your reply merely to agree with a board member

Frequently, a member will take a contrary position merely to draw you out and to see if you are willing and able to defend your point of view. Do not start a debate, yet do not surrender a good position. If a position is worth taking, it is worth defending.

14) Do not be afraid to admit an error in judgment if you are shown to be wrong

      The board knows that you are forced to reply without any opportunity for careful consideration. Your answer may be demonstrably wrong. If so, admit it and get on with the interview.

15) Do not dwell at length on your present job

      The opening question may relate to your present assignment. Answer the question but do not go into an extended discussion. You are being examined for a *new* job, not your present one. As a matter of fact, try to phrase ALL your answers in terms of the job for which you are being examined.

Basis of Rating

      Probably you will forget most of these "do's" and "don'ts" when you walk into the oral interview room. Even remembering them all will not ensure you a passing grade. Perhaps you did not have the qualifications in the first place. But remembering them will help you to put your best foot forward, without treading on the toes of the board members.

      Rumor and popular opinion to the contrary notwithstanding, an oral board wants you to make the best appearance possible. They know you are under pressure – but they also want to see how you respond to it as a guide to what your reaction would be under the pressures of the job you seek. They will be influenced by the degree of poise you display, the personal traits you show and the manner in which you respond.

ABOUT THIS BOOK

      This book contains tests divided into Examination Sections. Go through each test, answering every question in the margin. At the end of each test look at the answer key and check your answers. On the ones you got wrong, look at the right answer choice and learn. Do not fill in the answers first. Do not memorize the questions and answers, but understand the answer and principles involved. On your test, the questions will likely be different from the samples. Questions are changed and new ones added. If you understand these past questions you should have success with any changes that arise. Tests may consist of several types of questions. We have additional books on each subject should more study be advisable or necessary for you. Finally, the more you study, the better prepared you will be. This book is intended to be the last thing you study before you walk into the examination room. Prior study of relevant texts is also recommended. NLC publishes some of these in our Fundamental Series. Knowledge and good sense are important factors in passing your exam. Good luck also helps. So now study this Passbook, absorb the material contained within and take that knowledge into the examination. Then do your best to pass that exam.

———

EXAMINATION SECTION

EXAMINATION SECTION
TEST 1

DIRECTIONS: Each question or incomplete statement is followed by several suggested answers or completions. Select the one that BEST answers the question or completes the statement. *PRINT THE LETTER OF THE CORRECT ANSWER IN THE SPACE AT THE RIGHT.*

1. You attend a meeting where contentious issues will come up. To avoid any negative behavior, what should be done at the beginning of the gathering?
   A. Each side of the controversial issues should be heard
   B. A moderator should tell everyone that they do not expect to have both sides come to an agreement
   C. A neutral team member should make sure everyone agrees on facts involved with the problem
   D. Make sure your own side is heard before the other side gets a chance to speak

   1._____

2. E-mail is a large part of business communication. However, many e-mails are confusing or contain mistakes that lead to misunderstandings and misinterpretation. Of every 100 business-related e-mails, approximately how many are misunderstood by recipients?
   A. 10
   B. 20
   C. 50
   D. 90

   2._____

3. Which of the following is a disadvantage of using e-mail when communicating with employees?
   A. It is hard to put details into e-mails
   B. You cannot send them out to large groups of people
   C. It is quicker to hold a meeting than send out an e-mail
   D. It can be easy to misinterpret the tone of an e-mail

   3._____

4. In the communication process, a receiver is
   A. the person encoding a message
   B. a message pathway
   C. the person who decodes a message
   D. interference within a message

   4._____

5. One of your clients calls you and asks you to explain a confusing bylaw in one of his policies. What is the appropriate way to respond to him?
   A. Immediately transfer him to your manager
   B. Tell him to check the policy on your company's website
   C. Explain the policy in simpler terms and e-mail him a copy of the written policy
   D. Mail him a printed copy of the policy and tell him to read it for himself

   5._____

6. Your boss asks you to give a presentation to your coworkers. How can you   6._____
make sure they will remember the important parts of your production?
    A. Make sure your visual aids are "attention getters"
    B. Make humorous statements when you want the audience to
       remember something
    C. Allow the audience to ask questions about the important aspects
       of the presentation
    D. Summarize and stress your main ideas

7. Which of the following is important to keep in mind when preparing to make a   7._____
presentation?
    A. Audience interest and perspective
    B. Visual aids
    C. Charts and graphs
    D. Audience size

8. Why is customer feedback important to a company?   8._____
    A. It tells you if you are popular or not
    B. It lets you know if additional training is needed in certain areas
    C. It can help your company realize whether corporate policies need to be
       changed or not
    D. It informs you how the public feels about your company's ability to meet
       their needs

9. Your organization issued a press release and it is your job to post it on the   9._____
website for public viewing. This might require basic knowledge of
    A. Windows   B. FTP   C. HTML   D. HP

10. The managing director at your firm just made a significant error during his   10._____
keynote speech at a prestigious conference. This flawed statement could
mean a noteworthy loss to investors and other businesses. How should
Public Relations BEST handle this misstep?
    A. E-mail the corrected statement to anyone who attended
       the conference
    B. Put the corrected statement up on the company's website
    C. Train all Public Relations employees to answer questions
       about the issue
    D. Have the director publicly make a statement correcting his error
       and apologizing for the incorrect information

11. In order to meet deadlines, a supervisor should   11._____
    A. schedule work and stay informed on the progress of each task
    B. make sure he or she delegates the work properly
    C. hire temps when projects start to overwhelm regular staff
    D. have a good idea how capable each of your reliable employees are

12. One of your clients continually calls and complains that your staff members
are "a bunch of idiots" and a constant source of frustration.
What is the BEST way to deal with this situation?
    A. Keep quiet and let your client continue to rant until she calms down
    B. Tell her you will not speak to her until she stops using derogatory
       language toward your staff
    C. Attempt to steer the conversation towards the actual issue
       your client is having
    D. Tell your client they will need to speak with your manager

12._____

13. Your staff meetings constantly devolve into coworkers trying to push
different agendas and, as a result, nothing productive gets done. Your manager
asks you for input on how to solve this problem. What should she do?
    A. Tell all members to consider opening up to other priorities if
       they are logical
    B. Acknowledge the various opinions but attempt to focus on common
       goals and interests first
    C. Pretend everyone is on the same page and force everyone to
       get along or threaten them with termination
    D. Begin by allowing each member to speak about their priority then
       have everyone vote on which issues should be handled first

13._____

14. You go into a loan office to procure a loan of $1,000. They offer you the loan
with a 6% yearly interest. If you plan on paying off the loan in exactly one year,
how much will you pay back for the loan?
    A. $1,160.00   B. $1,016.67   C. $1,060.00   D. $166.67

14._____

15. You want to respond quickly to a client that is thinking about leaving for another
company's services. What is the FIRST thing you should do?
    A. Prepare an outline of what you want to say
    B. Brainstorm on possible reasons why they might want to leave
    C. Call them immediately and demand to know why they want to leave
    D. Decide on the approach that would be best to take with the customer to
       retain their loyalty

15._____

16. You are at a convention delivering a speech to company stakeholders.
During the Q&A session, one stakeholder makes a suggestion you think is
practical and valuable. How should you respond?
    A. Tell him the idea is worthwhile and promise to bring it to the
       appropriate person's attention
    B. Tell him it's a good idea and move on
    C. Tell him it's a good idea but you are not the person to talk to about it
    D. Tell him that someone in your company probably thought of that idea
       a long time ago

16._____

17. Sarah has the skills to do her job but her project teammates complain that   17._____
she is not working hard and therefore isn't doing her share.
The best response is to
    A. explain to her the standards and expectations of the job
    B. put her with a different team to see if anything changes
    C. give her a firm reprimand and tell her to get her act together
    D. fire her – you'll find someone else who won't take the job for granted

18. Which of the following would NOT be considered verbal communication?   18._____
    A. E-mail exchange
    B. Listening
    C. Telephone calls
    D. Text messaging

19. Feedback from a large number of customers indicates that many features of the   19._____
company website do not function as intended and are confusing in nature. After
reviewing the web features for yourself, you determine that the complaints are
accurate. What is the MOST appropriate immediate action to take?
    A. Set up a meeting between tech/web services and other necessary
       departments to determine what changes need to be made and when
    B. Inform the customers that the company is aware of the problems and will
       implement changes in next year's scheduled website update
    C. Demand an explanation from web services and an immediate overhaul of
       the website
    D. Provide customers with the name and phone number of a support contact

20. Which form of communication would be optimal if you wanted to talk to your   20._____
offices in Ireland, France and China at the same time?
    A. Video-conferencing
    B. Presentation
    C. Report
    D. E-mail

21. Which size of business is most likely to use informal communication more   21._____
regularly?
    A. Medium
    B. Large
    C. Small
    D. International

22. E-mails are effective when used to   22._____
    A. send long, complex information
    B. avoid confrontation
    C. exchange ideas
    D. discuss sensitive issues

23. If a customer calls needing someone to explain a policy that is complex in
nature, and you don't have the specific answers they are looking for,
what should you do?
    A. Give them as good of an answer as you can provide and hope
       that is enough
    B. Ask them to give you some time to find all the relevant information
       and tell them you'll call them back when you do
    C. Refer the caller to another more informed employee even if it means they
       will switch to that employee in the future
    D. Pretend to know the answers even if it means misleading your
       customer

23._____

24. Which of the following does NOT involve workplace communication?
    A. Answering customer letters
    B. Listening to instructions
    C. Lifting heavy boxes
    D. Working on team projects

24._____

25. Why is it important that one person does not dominate discussion during team
meetings?
    A. They may ramble which would make the meeting unbearably long
    B. Other team members may not get the chance to give their input
    C. Some members may lose focus and begin to daydream
    D. No one wants to hear the same voice for any length of time

25._____

KEY (CORRECT ANSWERS)

1. B	11. A	21. C
2. C	12. C	22. A
3. D	13. A	23. C
4. C	14. C	24. C
5. C	15. D	25. B
6. D	16. A	
7. A	17. A	
8. D	18. B	
9. C	19. A	
10. D	20. A	

TEST 2

DIRECTIONS: Each question or incomplete statement is followed by several suggested answers or completions. Select the one that BEST answers the question or completes the statement. *PRINT THE LETTER OF THE CORRECT ANSWER IN THE SPACE AT THE RIGHT.*

1. If a customer calls for information about a policy that is run by a rival business, what is the BEST way to respond?
   A. Tell them to check the other company's website
   B. Clarify that you are not responsible for the policy and therefore cannot comment
   C. Refer the caller to the other agency's office number
   D. Give them information to the best of your ability

   1._____

2. Which of the following is the MOST effective way to communicate during a speech?
   A. Prepare and memorize your script and stick to it throughout
   B. Speak with note cards you can reference throughout the speech
   C. Read the slides on your PowerPoint and try to make eye contact when you can
   D. Speak about whatever comes to your mind and don't worry about the note cards

   2._____

3. Your boss wants to send a message to office employees about a social event. She should send out a(n)
   A. agenda
   B. notice
   C. report
   D. fax

   3._____

4. Which of the following programs would be used to generate graphs and charts to be displayed in a public presentation?
   A. PowerPoint
   B. Photoshop
   C. Outlook
   D. Excel

   4._____

5. What should any good speaker avoid while making a presentation?
   A. Controversial issues
   B. Jargon
   C. Anything to do with finances or graphs
   D. Customer policies and/or company goals

   5._____

6. A new hire has been placed onto your team. What is the best way to help him succeed?
    6._____
    A. Let him try things out on his own and aid him if he asks
    B. Provide mentoring to help him learn
    C. Give him specific and detailed direction so he will not make any mistakes
    D. Work with him side by side

7. What should a public speaker do if they are confronted with a question to which they don't have a good answer?
    7._____
    A. Give an answer based on their comprehension of the topic
    B. Evade and try to focus the discussion on a topic you know better
    C. Tell them you have no idea how to answer the question
    D. Tell them you do not know the full answer to the question but you will find out and get back to them

8. Effective business communication
    8._____
    A. decreases the number of positive responses to requests on the first try
    B. increases reading time
    C. increases the time it takes disagreements to surface
    D. builds a positive image of your business

9. A customer sends your company a nasty complaint letter and you are in charge of responding. What is the BEST way to begin your response?
    9._____
    A. "I was given the task of replying to your complaint regarding our set of laws concerning Item #665349."
    B. "This is a letter to tell you we got your complaint concerning new policies on returns in regards to the item in question."
    C. "Hi, I am really glad you sent in your letter of complaint telling us what's wrong with our policies in connection with Item #665349."
    D. "Thank you for expressing your dissatisfaction with new policies in connection with your purchase (Item #665349)."

10. You are getting ready to write a memo correcting a fault made by your team. Which of the following MUST be included in the letter?
    10._____
    A. Details of why the error occurred
    B. A clear idea of exactly which team member is responsible for the fault
    C. Explanation of how this error will be fixed
    D. Excuses about how it is not really your team's fault because they are doing the best they can

11. Company X announced on its website that sales this year increased by 112%. If sales last year were $500,000, what amount are sales this year?
    11._____
    A. $512,000
    B. $560,000
    C. $1.06 million
    D. $1.6 million

12. Your boss wants to implement policy changes that could be unpopular among coworkers. He asks you how to best introduce these changes. What should you tell him?
    A. He should let people know what is happening and ask if they have feedback
    B. He should announce the policy changes without any warning and make it clear that employees need to accept the changes and adapt
    C. He should allow each employee to vote on all the separate policy changes. The only policy changes that will happen will be the ones that receive a majority vote.
    D. None of the above

12._____

13. If you ever have an irate customer who uses inflammatory language laced with obscenities, what is the BEST action to take?
    A. Tell them they need to calm down or you will discontinue the conversation
    B. Immediately transfer the call to your manager
    C. Let the customer finish his/her rant, then try to respond with a solution
    D. Hang up on the customer – your company doesn't need someone like that

13._____

14. Of the following, pick the one that doesn't fit with the others.
    A. Excel
    B. Gmail
    C. Yahoo
    D. Hotmail

14._____

15. Each person desires to be viewed positively by others, to be thought of favorably. This is referred to as maintaining
    A. positive face
    B. politeness
    C. abstraction
    D. negative face

15._____

16. A team member dominates every conversation she is involved in. As a team leader, how should you handle this situation?
    A. Refuse to let her speak until she learns how to listen
    B. Support other team members enthusiastically whenever they do speak up
    C. Stop the meeting and remind everyone to chip in with their opinions
    D. Privately discuss the issue with the team member in hopes of getting her to see why everyone should have a say

16._____

17. You are someone who gets really anxious when giving public speeches. Which of the following will NOT help you overcome your fears?
    A. Acknowledge your fears
    B. Avoid eye contact with audience members, that way it won't feel like they are there
    C. Act confident even if you don't feel it
    D. Channel your nervous energy into your speech

17._____

18. Which of the following would NOT be considered part of the setting for a public speech?   18._____
    A. Size of the audience
    B. Location of the speech
    C. If speech is held indoors or outdoors
    D. The length of the speech you're giving

19. Your boss tells you that a few of your employees have been complaining about your erratic methods of supervision. How should you respond?   19._____
    A. Tell your boss that you'll go to a supervisor training program
    B. Ask your boss if it was ethical for your employees to go over your head
    C. Ask your boss for specific acts that are considered inconsistent
    D. Explain that these few employees have made you inconsistent because of their neediness

20. Which of the following is NOT a purpose of giving a speech?   20._____
    A. To inform
    B. To entertain
    C. To persuade
    D. None of the above

21. Which of the following is an advantage of learning to effectively speak in public?   21._____
    A. Creating a message that can be understood by lots of people
    B. Convincing your audience of an important issue
    C. Inspiring your audience to take a certain action
    D. All of the above

22. Which of the following is NOT a reason that people fear speaking in public?   22._____
    A. They are perfectionists
    B. They are anxious about their future with the company
    C. They are overly prepared
    D. They tend to put off speech preparation until the last minute

23. Which of the following would be considered an external audience of a company?   23._____
    A. Peers
    B. Superiors
    C. Subordinates
    D. Stockholders

24. In preparation for a speech, what is important for you to know?   24._____
    A. The purpose of your speech
    B. The audience listening to your speech
    C. The time constraints of the speech
    D. All of the above

25. An employee in your department informs you that the company's monthly e-mail   25._____
newsletter was sent out to customers and subscribers with incorrect information.
As the head of the department, your first step in an effort to fix this mistake
should be to
    A. identify the person responsible and demand that they correct it
    B. assign someone in the department the task of developing a follow-up e-
        mail assuring customers that this sort of mistake will not occur again in
        future newsletters
    C. assign someone in the department the task of developing a follow-up e-
        mail that points out the error and contains corrected information
    D. inform the staff that you will be the only person to create and distribute
        future newsletters

———

KEY (CORRECT ANSWERS)

1. D	11. C	21. D
2. B	12. A	22. C
3. B	13. C	23. D
4. D	14. A	24. D
5. B	15. A	25. C
6. B	16. D	
7. D	17. B	
8. D	18. D	
9. D	19. C	
10. C	20. D	

———

EXAMINATION SECTION
TEST 1

DIRECTIONS: Each question or incomplete statement is followed by several suggested
answers or completions. Select the one that BEST answers the question or
completes the statement. *PRINT THE LETTER OF THE CORRECT ANSWER
IN THE SPACE AT THE RIGHT.*

1. Which of the following is NOT essential information that you need to know   1._____
   about your audience?
   A. How big the audience is
   B. What the audience is interested in
   C. What type of mood the audience is in
   D. If their attendance was mandatory or not

2. Which of the following is NOT one of the main reasons to communicate with   2._____
   the masses?
   A. Surveillance
   B. Entertainment
   C. Cultural transmission
   D. Correlation

3. Which of the following is true regarding e-mail?   3._____
   A. E-mail changes only the message
   B. E-mail changes only the way the message is delivered
   C. E-mail changes the way the message is delivered and the message itself
   D. E-mail changes neither the way the message is delivered nor the
      message itself

4. The best way to promote effective communication is   4._____
   A. practice good learning skills
   B. be aware of body language
   C. maintain eye contact
   D. all of the above

5. Before starting a speech, what should every public speaker make sure to do?   5._____
   A. Read through their notes really quickly
   B. Visualize their success in giving the speech
   C. Drink a lot of water so they are hydrated
   D. None of the above

6. The most important goal of business communication is   6._____
   A. a favorable relationship between speaker and listener
   B. administrative cohesion
   C. listener response
   D. listener understanding

7. Which of the following is an example of external communication?
    A. Meeting of employees in the purchasing department
    B. Telephone call from the area manager to the branch manager
    C. Letter from a supplier
    D. Discussion between a manager and an assistant

7._____

8. When introducing someone to an audience, which of the following should you avoid mentioning?
    A. Honors/accolades they received
    B. Recent or significant educational accomplishments
    C. Humor or jokes to lighten up the crowd
    D. Media attention or publications

8._____

9. Your office has organized a series of public events to prepare residents for the coming hurricane season. It is your job to inform attendees about the proper precautions to take when securing their homes and protecting their belongings in the event of a major storm. The BEST way to do this is to
    A. hand out detailed brochures and answer questions while experts demonstrate appropriate methods and procedures
    B. distribute brochures as well as pamphlets with information on how to view demonstrations on your office's YouTube channel
    C. give out magnets and paperweights containing a URL link to a storm-preparation website
    D. hand out storm-readiness pamphlets at the entrance along with a voucher for a free popcorn and soda

9._____

10. Which of the following would NOT be considered part of project management?
    A. A clearly stated objective
    B. A timeline for beginning and ending the project
    C. Complex tasks and/or intricate teamwork
    D. None of the above

10._____

11. What is the best way to recognize an employee who has gone above and beyond their job expectations?
    A. Celebrate his success with the whole team or group
    B. Take him out to a one-on-one lunch and tell him how special he is
    C. Ask him what sort of extra benefit or reward he would like for doing such a great job
    D. Give him a "Thank You" card signed by his coworkers

11._____

12. Your friend has been supervising a group of people for the last 18 months.   12._____
He tells you that in this time, none of his employees reported any problems to
him. He asks you if you think this is a problem. You should tell him
   - A. he is doing great and there is no room for improvement
   - B. his staff is relatively small, so the chance of problems arising are smaller
      than if he had a larger group
   - C. his staff may be reluctant to discuss problems with him so he should ask
      them if there are any concerns
   - D. his employees are competent and are handling their problems well by
      themselves.

13. Which of the following BEST describes a physiological noise?   13._____
   - A. Weed whacker
   - B. Air conditioner
   - C. Listener reviewing their to-do list while you're speaking
   - D. A speaker using complex terms

14. The ability to feel compassion and understanding for another person's situation is   14._____
   - A. empathy
   - B. common sense
   - C. professionalism
   - D. audience analysis

15. A longtime employee suddenly starts coming in late to work a couple of times   15._____
each week. What is the best approach to solve this problem?
   - A. Tell coworkers to talk to the employee to see what is going on
   - B. Meet with the employee to tell her she needs to stop coming in late
   - C. Dock her pay and tell her if it doesn't stop she will be fired
   - D. All of the above

16. You are in a meeting with your boss and a representative from a company that   16._____
your team does business with. During the meeting, the representative hands you
and your supervisor an expensive watch, which your boss eagerly accepts. What
should you do?
   - A. Accept the gift – your boss approves
   - B. Refuse the gift – your supervisor's acceptance does not mean
      the company approves of the gift
   - C. Accept the gift and then give it to a friend later – this way you
      don't make a scene
   - D. Accept the gift as long as the representative knows that it won't
      give him any preferential treatment

17. In the interviews for a vacant clerical position, none of the job candidates have all   17._____
the skills necessary to do the job competently. Which candidate would be the
BEST option for your company?
    A. Marianne, who has no formal education and says she can do the
        job based on her related work experience
    B. Jason, who has no related experience but lots of enthusiasm to learn
        to do the job
    C. Gillian, who has completed a related training program but has
        no experience
    D. None of the above – re-advertise and find more qualified help

18. Which of the following would benefit the most from strong project management?   18._____
    A. Processing an insurance claim
    B. Making an automobile
    C. Writing an essay
    D. Finishing a college degree

19. During the _____ stage, objectives are stated, the team is put together, and   19._____
responsibilities are assigned.
    A. conceptualization
    B. definition
    C. planning
    D. execution

20. Which of the following is the most widely used source of information about   20._____
events currently happening in the world?
    A. TV
    B. Radio
    C. Newspapers
    D. Professional journals

21. A customer complained to your supervisor because during a conversation about   21._____
water conservation, you said it was "idiotic" for people to let hoses run when not
in use. A more acceptable term would have been
    A. reckless
    B. moronic
    C. irresponsible
    D. mind-boggling

22. Your supervisor reprimands a worker for his neglect of duty, but he does it in a   22._____
very public and embarrassing way. Which of the following would have been
the best action for your supervisor to take?
    A. Tell the employee about the neglect but in a private meeting
    B. Tell the employee about his good points and downplay the bad in private
    C. Allow the employee to begin with a clean record by avoiding criticism
    D. Nothing was wrong with how your supervisor handled the situation

23. Verbal and nonverbal responses to a message are called   23._____
    A. nonverbal code
    B. verbal code
    C. feedback
    D. external interference

24. One of your coworkers is involved in an increasingly animated conversation with 24._____
a client. You intervene, and the coworker says he's trying to explain a company
policy and doesn't appreciate the client's dismissive body language. Which of
the following actions by the client might be the cause of the tension?
    A. Constant interrupting during the explanation
    B. Lack of eye contact
    C. A derisive sneer or hand gesture when he doesn't like the explanation
    D. Evading questions

25. You are in a customer service job and someone with a speech impairment   25._____
has called you. What is the most effective way to communicate with them?
    A. Repeat his answer back to his to make sure you understood what he said
    B. Give him as much time as he needs to finish his statements
    C. Try to finish his sentences if he seems to struggle
    D. Try to make the conversation as short as possible so it won't be awkward

KEY (CORRECT ANSWERS)

1. D	11. A	21. C
2. A	12. C	22. A
3. B	13. C	23. C
4. D	14. A	24. C
5. B	15. B	25. B
6. A	16. B	
7. C	17. D	
8. C	18. B	
9. A	19. C	
10. D	20. A	

TEST 2

DIRECTIONS: Each question or incomplete statement is followed by several suggested answers or completions. Select the one that BEST answers the question or completes the statement. *PRINT THE LETTER OF THE CORRECT ANSWER IN THE SPACE AT THE RIGHT.*

1. If you are interacting with a customer who is not speaking, which of the following would be considered negative body language that they are sending to you?
    A. Facing you while you're talking
    B. If they roll their eyes at you
    C. If they are sitting in a relaxed position
    D. If they maintain eye contact

    1._____

2. Which of the following is NOT a barrier to communicating in an effective manner?
    A. Interrupting someone who is speaking to you
    B. Complaining too much while speaking to a coworker
    C. Obscuring your face with your hand or a piece of paper
    D. Making a broad opening statement

    2._____

3. A client requests a photo of a recent meeting. Which of the following types of files would you NOT send?
    A. .jpg
    B. .tif
    C. .png
    D. .mov

    3._____

4. Although accuracy and speed are both vital in work performance, accuracy is more important because
    A. most supervisors insist on accurate work
    B. too much time is lost in correcting errors
    C. rapid work rates cannot be maintained for any real length of time
    D. speedy workers are too inaccurate

    4._____

5. You recently gave an interview to a local television news reporter about measures the town government is taking to improve playground safety. Community feedback has been almost entirely negative.
What is a likely reason for this type of feedback?
    A. Important information was left out in favor of promotion of unrelated town programs and events
    B. Delivery of information was slow and measured
    C. The reporter's questions were very direct
    D. The safety program is a waste of taxpayer money

    5._____

6. Your department was responsible for a local barbecue and volleyball tournament   6._____
   that raised more than $10,000 for cancer research. Feedback from attendees
   and local businesses was overwhelmingly positive, and many stated their interest
   in participating again next year. However, in the comments section associated
   with an Internet newspaper article about the event, several anonymous users
   said the event was a waste of money, the food was terrible and the volleyball
   referees were biased. Some users also made derogatory statements about
   people in the event photos.
   As one of the organizers of the event, you should
   - A. ignore the comments – direct feedback from the community was positive,
        and the opinions of anonymous commenters have no value
   - B. have the newspaper publish a full-page ad thanking the community for its
        support
   - C. demand that the newspaper remove negative commentary as it might hurt
        the success of next year's event
   - D. respond directly to the commenters to help them understand the
        importance of the fundraiser

7. What is implied by the statement, "Communication is a process"?   7._____
   - A. There is a clear beginning and end point to it
   - B. Communication more closely resembles a photo rather than a movie
   - C. Communication is continuous and ongoing
   - D. None of the above

8. You need your employees to work overtime. Which of the following would   8._____
   be the best way to break the news?
   - A. Tell them you'd consider it a personal favor for them to work overtime
   - B. Tell them why the overtime is necessary
   - C. Reassure them that they can take time off in the future
   - D. Remind them that working overtime is part of their job description

9. A specific behavior may be acceptable in one situation and inappropriate   9._____
   in another. This example best illustrates the idea that communication aptitude
   - A. includes choosing poor behaviors
   - B. includes being combative
   - C. includes being extremely intelligent
   - D. is situational

10. You are training at your new job and you spend today learning about the forms   10._____
    and paperwork used by the company in customer relations. What area of
    training would this fall under?
    - A. Interpersonal skills
    - B. Customer knowledge
    - C. Technical skills
    - D. Product and service knowledge

11. If you need to revise and edit a document for your boss, you should   11._____
    A. spell and grammar check on the computer
    B. read the draft out loud
    C. quick-read the draft.
    D. analyze the draft in one reading

12. Which of the following is an example of self-monitoring?   12._____
    A. Having a checklist to refer to for skills to practice
    B. Listening to your own voice while speaking with others
    C. Watching others react to your jokes
    D. All of the above

13. A tractor driving by and interfering with your conversation is an example of   13._____
    what kind of noise?
    A. External
    B. Psychological
    C. Psychological
    D. Internal

14. It is casual Friday and your boss disapproves of the music group pictured on   14._____
    your shirt. His attitude toward you in your staff meeting is frosty and distant.
    This is an example of what kind of communication distraction?
    A. External
    B. Psychological
    C. Physiological
    D. Internal

15. In the majority of situations, proficient communicators can   15._____
    A. choose from a wide variety of behaviors
    B. demonstrate empathy
    C. use self-monitoring to improve their communication skills
    D. all of the above

16. Mass communication usually tends to be   16._____
    A. one way
    B. communication from one to many
    C. anonymous
    D. none of the above

17. When communicating, to encode a message means   17._____
    A. speaking to large groups of people
    B. blocking a pathway between the sender and receiver of a message
    C. translate an idea into coded message
    D. interpret a coded message

18. Which of the following is a way to provide feedback when communicating?   18._____
    A. Verbally
    B. Nonverbally
    C. Through environmental noise
    D. Verbally and nonverbally from the listener

19. When creating a vacation schedule for your employees, which of the following is   19._____
    least important to consider?
    A. Employee proficiency
    B. Employee preference
    C. Anticipated workload for each quarter
    D. How pertinent each employee's services are during each vacation period

20. When thinking about the range and scope of an e-mail, you should consider   20._____
    A. the amount of detail needed in the message
    B. how technical the document should be
    C. what format the audience expects
    D. all of the above

21. You discover that one of your colleagues has received bribes from a business   21._____
    to make sure their bid for a project is accepted. What should you do?
    A. Pretend that you didn't hear anything and do nothing
    B. Report it to management
    C. Ask your colleague to stop his unethical behavior
    D. Ask your manager to be transferred to a different department

22. If the person you are talking to has a hearing problem that is causing a   22._____
    communication barrier between the two of you, what should you do to help
    overcome this barrier?
    A. Find someone who knows sign language
    B. Learn sign language yourself
    C. Speak louder or put your message in writing
    D. Suggest to the person that they need to get medical attention

23. When a supervisor assigns work to his team members, which of the following   23._____
    criteria would be the best for them to use?
    A. Allow each employee to choose which tasks he or she is the best at
    B. Assign the more difficult work to newer team members
    C. Give any tedious/unimportant work to slower employees
    D. Delegate assignments based on the abilities of employees

24. Which of the following is true of writing skills for a professional in the workplace?   24._____
    A. They are rarely used because the Internet makes writing unnecessary
    B. They are not required because secretaries do most of the writing for
       professionals
    C. They are important but not essential because many pre-designed
       templates are available to use
    D. They are a key job requirement and are frequently listed in professional
       job descriptions

25. The method of writers working together to create memos, letters or other business documents is called _____ writing.
    A. choreographed
    B. combative
    C. collaborative
    D. coalesced

25._____

KEY (CORRECT ANSWERS)

1. B	11. B	21. B
2. D	12. D	22. A
3. D	13. A	23. D
4. A	14. B	24. D
5. A	15. D	25. C
6. A	16. B	
7. C	17. C	
8. C	18. D	
9. D	19. A	
10. C	20. D	

EXAMINATION SECTION
TEST 1

DIRECTIONS: Each question or incomplete statement is followed by several suggested answers or completions. Select the one that BEST answers the question or completes the statement. *PRINT THE LETTER OF THE CORRECT ANSWER IN THE SPACE AT THE RIGHT.*

1. When conducting a needs assessment for the purpose of education planning, an agency's FIRST step is to identify or provide
    A. a profile of population characteristics
    B. barriers to participation
    C. existing resources
    D. profiles of competing resources

1.____

2. Research has demonstrated that of the following, the MOST effective medium for communicating with external publics is(are)
    A. video news releases   B. television
    C. radio   D. newspapers

2.____

3. Basic ideas behind the effort to influence the attitudes and behaviors of a constituency include each of the following EXCEPT the idea that
    A. words, rather than actions or events, are most likely to motivate
    B. demands for action are a usual response
    C. self-interest usually figures heavily into public involvement
    D. the reliability of change programs is difficult to assess

3.____

4. An agency representative is trying to craft a pithy message to constituents in order to encourage the use of agency program resources.
    Choosing an audience for such messages is easiest when the message
    A. is project- or behavior-based   B. is combined with other messages
    C. is abstract   D. has a broad appeal

4.____

5. Of the following factors, the MOST important to the success of an agency's external education or communication programs is the
    A. amount of resources used to implement them
    B. public's prior experiences with the agency
    C. real value of the program to the public
    D. commitment of the internal audience

5.____

6. A representative for a state agency is being interviewed by a reporter from a local news network. The representative is being asked to defend a program that is extremely unpopular in certain parts of the municipality.
    When a constituency is known to be opposed to a position, the MOST useful communication strategy is to present

6.____

A. only the arguments that are consistent with constituents' views
B. only the agency's side of the issue
C. both sides of the argument as clearly as possible
D. both sides of the argument, omitting key information about the opposing
    position

7. The MOST significant barriers to effective agency community relations include   7.____
    I.   widespread distrust of communication strategies
    II. the media's "watchdog" stance
    III. public apathy
    IV. statutory opposition

    The CORRECT answer is:
    A. I only   B. I and II   C. II and III   D. III and IV

8. In conducting an education program, many agencies use workshops and   8.____
    seminars in a classroom setting.
    Advantages of classroom-style teaching over other means of educating the
    public include each of the following, EXCEPT
    A. enabling an instructor to verify learning through testing and interaction
        with the target audience
    B. enabling hands-on practice and other participatory learning techniques
    C. ability to reach an unlimited number of participants in a given length of
        time
    D. ability to convey the latest, most up-to-date information

9. The _____ model of community relations is characterized by an attempt to   9.____
    persuade the public to adopt the agency's point of view.
    A. two-way symmetric   B. two-way asymmetric
    C. public information   D. press agency/publicity

10. Important elements of an internal situation analysis include the   10.____
    I.   list of agency opponents   II. communication audit
    III. updated organizational almanac IV. stakeholder analysis

    The CORRECT answer is:
    A. I and II   B. I, II, and III   C. II and III   D. I, II, III and IV

11. Government agency information efforts typically involve each of the following   11.____
    objectives, EXCEPT to
    A. implement changes in the policies of government agencies to align with
        public opinion
    B. communicate the work of agencies
    C. explain agency techniques in a way that invites input from citizens
    D. provide citizen feedback to government administrators

12. Factors that are likely to influence the effectiveness of an educational campaign include the
    I. level of homogeneity among intended participants
    II. number and types of media used
    III. receptivity of the intended participants
    IV. level of specificity in the message or behavior to be taught

    The CORRECT answer is:
    A. I and II   B. I, II, and III   C. II and III   D. I, II, III, and IV

12.____

13. An agency representative is writing instructional objectives that will later help to measure the effectiveness of an educational program.
    Which of the following verbs, included in an objective, would be MOST helpful for the purpose of measuring effectiveness?
    A. Know   B. Identify   C. Learn   D. Comprehend

13.____

14. A state education agency wants to encourage participation in a program that has just received a boost through new federal legislation. The program is intended to include participants from a wide variety of socioeconomic and other demographic characteristics. The agency wants to launch a broad-based program that will inform virtually every interested party in the state about the program's new circumstances.
    In attempting to deliver this message to such a wide-ranging constituency, the agency's BEST practice would be to
    A. broadcast the same message through as many different media channels as possible
    B. focus on one discrete segment of the public at a time
    C. craft a message whose appeal is as broad as the public itself
    D. let the program's achievements speak for themselves and rely on word-of-mouth

14.____

15. Advantages associated with using the World Wide Web as an educational tool include
    I. an appeal to younger generations of the public
    II. visually-oriented, interactive learning
    III. learning that is not confined by space, time, or institutional association
    IV. a variety of methods for verifying use and learning

    The CORRECT answer is:
    A. I only   B. I and II   C. I, II, and III   D. I, II, II, and IV

15.____

16. In agencies involved in health care, community relations is a critical function because it
    A. serves as an intermediary between the agency and consumers
    B. generates a clear mission statement for agency goals and priorities
    C. ensures patient privacy while satisfying the media's right to information
    D. helps marketing professionals determine the wants and needs of agency constituents

16.____

17. After an extensive campaign to promote its newest program to constituents, an agency learns that most of the audience did not understand the intended message.
    MOST likely, the agency has
    A. chosen words that were intended to inform, rather than persuade
    B. not accurately interpreted what the audience really needed to know
    C. overestimated the ability of the audience to receive and process the message
    D. compensated for noise that may have interrupted the message

17._____

18. The necessary elements that lead to conviction and motivation in the minds of participants in an educational or information program include each of the following, EXCEPT the _____ of the message.
    A. acceptability   B. intensity
    C. single-channel appeal   D. pervasiveness

18._____

19. Printed materials are often at the core of educational programs provided by public agencies.
    The PRIMARY disadvantage associated with print is that it
    A. does not enable comprehensive treatment of a topic
    B. is generally unreliable in term of assessing results
    C. is often the most expensive medium available
    D. is constrained by time

19._____

20. Traditional thinking on public opinion holds that there is about _____ percent of the public who are pivotal to shifting the balance and momentum of opinion—they are concerned about an issue, but not fanatical, and interested enough to pay attention to a reasoned discussion.
    A. 2   B. 10   C. 33   D. 51

20._____

21. One of the most useful guidelines for influencing attitude change among people is to
    A. invite the target audience to come to you, rather than approaching them
    B. use moral appeals as the primary approach
    C. use concrete images to enable people to see the results of behaviors or indifference
    D. offer tangible rewards to people for changes in behavior

21._____

22. An agency is attempting to evaluate the effectiveness of its educational program. For this purpose, it wants to observe several focus groups discussing the same program.
    Which of the following would NOT be a guideline for the use of focus groups?
    A. Focus groups should only include those who have participated in the program.
    B. Be sure to accurately record the discussion.
    C. The same questions should be asked at each focus group meeting.
    D. It is often helpful to have a neutral, non-agency employee facilitate discussions.

22._____

23. Research consistently shows that _____ is the determinant most likely to make a newspaper editor run a news release.
    A. novelty   B. prominence   C. proximity   D. conflict

23.____

24. Which of the following is NOT one of the major variables to take into account when considering a population-needs assessment?
    A. State of program development   B. Resources available
    C. Demographics   D. Community attitudes

24.____

25. The FIRST step in any communications audit is to
    A. develop a research instrument
    B. determine how the organization currently communicates
    C. hire a contractor
    D. determine which audience to assess

25.____

KEY (CORRECT ANSWERS)

1.	A		11.	A
2.	D		12.	D
3.	A		13.	B
4.	A		14.	B
5.	D		15.	C
6.	C		16.	A
7.	D		17.	B
8.	C		18.	C
9.	B		19.	B
10.	C		20.	B

21. C
22. A
23. C
24. C
25. D

TEST 2

DIRECTIONS: Each question or incomplete statement is followed by several suggested answers or completions. Select the one that BEST answers the question or completes the statement. *PRINT THE LETTER OF THE CORRECT ANSWER IN THE SPACE AT THE RIGHT.*

1. A public relations practitioner at an agency has just composed a press release highlighting a program's recent accomplishments and success stories.
   In pitching such releases to print outlets, the practitioner should
   I.   e-mail, mail, or send them by messenger
   II. address them to "editor" or "news director"
   III. have an assistant call all media contacts by telephone
   IV. ask reporters or editors how they prefer to receive them

   The CORRECT answer is:
   A. I and II   B. I and IV   C. II, III, and IV   D. III only

   1.____

2. The "output goals" of an educational program are MOST likely to include
   A. specified ratings of services by participants on a standardized scale
   B. observable effects on a given community or clientele
   C. the number of instructional hours provided
   D. the number of participants served

   2.____

3. An agency wants to evaluate satisfaction levels among program participants, and mails out questionnaires to everyone who has been enrolled in the last year.
   The PRIMARY problem associated with this method of evaluative research is that it
   A. poses a significant inconvenience for respondents
   B. is inordinately expensive
   C. does not allow for follow-up or clarification questions
   D. usually involves a low response rate

   3.____

4. A communications audit is an important tool for measuring
   A. the depth of penetration of a particular message or program
   B. the cost of the organization's information campaigns
   C. how key audiences perceive an organization
   D. the commitment of internal stakeholders

   4.____

5. The "ABCs" of written learning objectives include each of the following, EXCEPT
   A. Audience   B. Behavior   C. Conditions   D. Delineation

   5.____

6. When attempting to change the behaviors of constituents, it is important to keep in mind that
   I. most people are skeptical of communications that try to get them to change their behaviors
   II. in most cases, a person selects the media to which he exposes himself
   III. people tend to react defensively to messages or programs that rely on fear as a motivating factor
   IV. programs should aim for the broadest appeal possible in order to include as many participants as possible

   The CORRECT answer is:
   A. I and II   B. I, II and III   C. II and III   D. I, II, III, and IV

6.____

7. The "laws" of public opinion include the idea that it is
   A. useful for anticipating emergencies
   B. not sensitive to important events
   C. basically determined by self-interest
   D. sustainable through persistent appeals

7.____

8. Which of the following types of evaluations is used to measure public attitudes before and after an information/educational program?
   A. Retrieval study   B. Copy test
   C. Quota sampling   D. Benchmark study

8.____

9. The PRIMARY source for internal communications is(are) usually
   A. flow charts   B. meetings
   C. voice mail   D. printed publications

9.____

10. An agency representative is putting together informational materials—brochures and a newsletter—outlining changes in one of the state's biggest benefits programs.
   In assembling print materials as a medium for delivering information to the public, the representative should keep in mind each of the following trends:
   I. For various reasons, the reading capabilities of the public are in general decline
   II. Without tables and graphs to help illustrate the changes, it is unlikely that the message will be delivered effectively
   III. Professionals and career-oriented people are highly receptive to information written in the form of a journal article or empirical study
   IV. People tend to be put off by print materials that use itemized and bulleted (●) lists

   The CORRECT answer is:
   A. I and II   B. I, II and III   C. II and III   D. I, II, III, and IV

10.____

11. Which of the following steps in a problem-oriented information campaign would typically be implemented FIRST?
    A. Deciding on tactics
    B. Determining a communications strategy
    C. Evaluating the problem's impact
    D. Developing an organizational strategy

11.____

12. A common pitfall in conducting an educational program is to
    A. aim it at the wrong target audience
    B. overfund it
    C. leave it in the hands of people who are in the business of education, rather than those with expertise in the business of the organization
    D. ignore the possibility that some other organization is meeting the same educational need for the target audience

12.____

13. The key factors that affect the credibility of an agency's educational program include
    A. organization   B. scope
    C. sophistication   D. penetration

13.____

14. Research on public opinion consistently demonstrates that it is
    A. easy to move people toward a strong opinion on anything, as long as they are approached directly through their emotions
    B. easier to move people away from an opinion they currently hold than to have them form an opinion about something they have not previously cared about
    C. easy to move people toward a strong opinion on anything, as long as the message appeals to their reason and intellect
    D. difficult to move people toward a strong opinion on anything, no matter what the approach

14.____

15. In conducting an education program, many agencies use meetings and conferences to educate an audience about the organization and its programs. Advantages associated with this approach include
    I. a captive audience that is known to be interested in the topic
    II. ample opportunities for verifying learning
    III. cost-efficient meeting space
    IV. the ability to provide information on a wider variety of subjects

    The CORRECT answer is:
    A. I and II   B. I, III and IV   C. II and III   D. I, II, III and IV

15.____

16. An agency is attempting to evaluate the effectiveness of its educational programs. For this purpose, it wants to observe several focus groups discussing particular programs.
    For this purpose, a focus group should never number more than _____ participants.
    A. 5   B. 10   C. 15   D. 20

16.____

28

17. A _____ speech is written so that several agency members can deliver it to different audiences with only minor variations.
    A. basic   B. printed   C. quota   D. pattern

17._____

18. Which of the following statements about public opinion is generally considered to be FALSE?
    A. Opinion is primarily reactive rather than proactive.
    B. People have more opinions about goals than about the means by which to achieve them.
    C. Facts tend to shift opinion in the accepted direction when opinion is not solidly structured.
    D. Public opinion is based more on information than desire.

18._____

19. An agency is trying to promote its educational program.
    As a general rule, the agency should NOT assume that
    A. people will only participate if they perceive an individual benefit
    B. promotions need to be aimed at small, discrete groups
    C. if the program is good, the audience will find out about it
    D. a variety of methods, including advertising, special events, and direct mail, should be considered

19._____

20. In planning a successful educational program, probably the first and most important question for an agency to ask is:
    A. What will be the content of the program?
    B. Who will be served by the program?
    C. When is the best time to schedule the program?
    D. Why is the program necessary?

20._____

21. Media kits are LEAST likely to contain
    A. fact sheets   B. memoranda
    C. photographs with captions   D. news releases

21._____

22. The use of pamphlets and booklets as media for communication with the public often involves the disadvantage that
    A. the messages contained within them are frequently nonspecific
    B. it is difficult to measure their effectiveness in delivering the message
    C. there are few opportunities for people to refer to them
    D. color reproduction is poor

22._____

23. The MOST important prerequisite of a good educational program is an
    A. abundance of resources to implement it
    B. individual staff unit formed for the purpose of program delivery
    C. accurate needs assessment
    D. uneducated constituency

23._____

29

24. After an education program has been delivered, an agency conducts a program   24.____
evaluation to determine whether its objectives have been met.
General rules about how to conduct such an education program valuation
include each of the following, EXCEPT that it
    A. must be done immediately after the program has been implemented
    B. should be simple and easy to use
    C. should be designed so that tabulation of responses can take place quickly
       and inexpensively
    D. should solicit mostly subjective, open-ended responses if the audience
       was large

25. Using electronic media such as television as means of educating the public   25.____
is typically recommended ONLY for agencies that
    I.   have a fairly simple message to begin with
    II. want to reach the masses, rather than a targeted audience
    III. have substantial financial resources
    IV. accept that they will not be able to measure the results of the campaign
        with much precision

The CORRECT answer is:
    A. I and II   B. I, II and III   C. II and IV   D. I, II, III and IV

KEY (CORRECT ANSWERS)

1.	B		11.	C
2.	C		12.	D
3.	D		13.	A
4.	C		14.	D
5.	D		15.	B
6.	B		16.	B
7.	C		17.	D
8.	D		18.	D
9.	D		19.	C
10.	A		20.	D

21.	B
22.	B
23.	C
24.	D
25.	D

EXAMINATION SECTION
TEST 1

DIRECTIONS: Each question or incomplete statement is followed by several suggested answers or completions. Select the one that BEST answers the question or completes the statement. *PRINT THE LETTER OF THE CORRECT ANSWER IN THE SPACE AT THE RIGHT.*

1. In public agencies, communications should be based PRIMARILY on a
   A. two-way flow from the top down and from the bottom up, most of which should be given in writing to avoid ambiguity
   B. multi-direction flow among all levels and with outside persons
   C. rapid, internal one-way flow from the top down
   D. two-way flow of information, most of which should be given orally for purposes of clarity

   1.____

2. In some organizations, changes in policy or procedures are often communicated by word of mouth from supervisors to employees with no prior discussion or exchange of viewpoints with employees.
   This procedure often produces employee dissatisfaction CHIEFLY because
   A. information is mostly unusable since a considerable amount of time is required to transmit information
   B. lower-level supervisors tend to be excessively concerned with minor details
   C. management has failed to seek employees' advice before making changes
   D. valuable staff time is lost between decision-making and the implementation of decisions

   2.____

3. For good letter writing, you should try to visualize the person to whom you are writing, especially if you know him.
   Of the following rules, it is LEAST helpful in such visualization to think of
   A. the person's likes and dislikes, his concerns, and his needs
   B. what you would be likely to say if speaking in person
   C. what you would expect to be asked if speaking in person
   D. your official position in order to be certain that your words are proper

   3.____

4. One approach to good informal letter writing is to make letters and conversational.
   All of the following practices will usually help to do this EXCEPT:
   A. If possible, use a style which is similar to the style used when speaking
   B. Substitute phrases for single words (e.g., *at the present time* for *now*)
   C. Use contractions of words (e.g., *you're* for *you are*)
   D. Use ordinary vocabulary when possible

   4.____

5. All of the following rules will aid in producing clarity in report-writing EXCEPT: 5.____
   A. Give specific details or examples, if possible
   B. Keep related words close together in each sentence
   C. Present information in sequential order
   D. Put several thoughts or ideas in each paragraph

6. The one of the following statements about public relations which is MOST   6.____
   accurate is that
   A. in the long run, appearance gains better results than performance
   B. objectivity is decreased if outside public relations consultants are
      employed
   C. public relations is the responsibility of every employee
   D. public relations should be based on a formal publicity program

7. The form of communication which is usually considered to be MOST personally   7.____
   directed to the intended recipient is the
   A. brochure   B. film   C. letter   D. radio

8. In general, a document that presents an organization's views or opinions   8.____
   on a particular topic is MOST accurately known as a
   A. tear sheet   B. position paper
   C. flyer   D. journal

9. Assume that you have been asked to speak before an organization of persons   9.____
   who oppose a newly announced program in which you are involved. You feel
   tense about talking to this group.
   Which of the following rules generally would be MOST useful in gaining rapport
   when speaking before the audience?
   A. Impress them with your experience
   B. Stress all areas of disagreement
   C. Talk to the group as to one person
   D. Use formal grammar and language

10. An organization must have an effective public relations program since, at its   10.____
    best, public relations is a bridge to change.
    All of the following statements about communication and human behavior have
    validity EXCEPT:
    A. People are more likely to talk about controversial matters with like-minded
       people than with those holding other views
    B. The earlier an experience, the more powerful its effect since it influences
       how later experiences will be interpreted
    C. In periods of social tension, official sources gain increased believability
    D. Those who are already interested in a topic are the ones who are most
       open to receive new communications about it

11. An employee should be encouraged to talk easily and frankly when he is dealing with his supervisor.
    In order to encourage such free communication, it would be MOST appropriate for a supervisor to behave in a(n)
    A. sincere manner; assure the employee that you will deal with him honestly and openly
    B. official manner; you are a supervisor and must always act formally with subordinates
    C. investigative manner; you must probe and question to get to a basis of trust
    D. unemotional manner; the employee's emotions and background should play no part in your dealings with him

11.____

12. Research findings show that an increase in free communication within an agency GENERALLY results in which one of the following?
    A. Improved morale and productivity
    B. Increased promotional opportunities
    C. An increase in authority
    D. A spirit of honesty

12.____

13. Assume that you are a supervisor and your superiors have given you a new-type procedure to be followed.
    Before passing this information on to your subordinates, the one of the following actions that you should take FIRST is to
    A. ask your superiors to send out a memorandum to the entire staff
    B. clarify the procedure in your own mind
    C. set up a training course to provide instruction on the new procedure
    D. write a memorandum to your subordinates

13.____

14. Communication is necessary for an organization to be effective.
    The one of the following which is LEAST important for most communication systems is that
    A. messages are sent quickly and directly to the person who needs them to operate
    B. information should be conveyed understandably and accurately
    C. the method used to transmit information should be kept secret so that security can be maintained
    D. senders of messages must know how their messages are received and acted upon

14.____

15. Which one of the following is the CHIEF advantage of listening willingly to subordinates and encouraging them to talk freely and honestly?
    It
    A. reveals to supervisors the degree to which ideas that are passed down are accepted by subordinates
    B. reduces the participation of subordinates in the operation of the department
    C. encourages subordinates to try for promotion
    D. enables supervisors to learn more readily what the *grapevine* is saying

15.____

16. A supervisor may be informed through either oral or written reports.
    Which one of the following is an ADVANTAGE of using oral reports?
    A. There is no need for a formal record of the report.
    B. An exact duplicate of the report is not easily transmitted to others.
    C. A good oral report requires little time for preparation.
    D. An oral report involves two-way communication between a subordinate and his supervisor.

16.____

17. Of the following, the MOST important reason why supervisors should communicate effectively with the public is to
    A. improve the public's understanding of information that is important for them to know
    B. establish a friendly relationship
    C. obtain information about the kinds of people who come to the agency
    D. convince the public that services are adequate

17.____

18. Supervisors should generally NOT use phrases like *too hard*, *too easy*, and *a lot* PRINCIPALLY because such phrases
    A. may be offensive to some minority groups
    B. are too informal
    C. mean different things to different people
    D. are difficult to remember

18.____

19. The ability to communicate clearly and concisely is an important element in effective leadership.
    Which of the following statements about oral and written communication is GENERALLY true?
    A. Oral communication is more time-consuming.
    B. Written communication is more likely to be misinterpreted.
    C. Oral communication is useful only in emergencies.
    D. Written communication is useful mainly when giving information to fewer than twenty people.

19.____

20. Rumors can often have harmful and disruptive effects on an organization.
    Which one of the following is the BEST way to prevent rumors from becoming a problem?
    A. Refuse to act on rumors, thereby making them less believable.
    B. Increase the amount of information passed along by the *grapevine*.
    C. Distribute as much factual information as possible.
    D. Provide training in report writing.

20.____

21. Suppose that a subordinate asks you about a rumor he has heard. The rumor deals with a subject which your superiors consider *confidential*.
    Which of the following BEST describes how you should answer the subordinate? Tell

21.____

A. the subordinate that you don't make the rules and that he should speak to higher ranking officials
B. the subordinate that you will ask your superior for information
C. him only that you cannot comment on the matter
D. him the rumor is not true

22. Supervisors often find it difficult to *get their message across* when instructing newly appointed employees in their various duties.
The MAIN reason for this is generally that the
    A. duties of the employees have increased
    B. supervisor is often so expert in his area that he fails to see it from the learner's point of view
    C. supervisor adapts his instruction to the slowest learner in the group
    D. new employees are younger, less concerned with job security and more interested in fringe benefits

22.____

23. Assume that you are discussing a job problem with an employee under your supervision. During the discussion, you see that the man's eyes are turning away from you and that he is not paying attention.
In order to get the man's attention, you should FIRST
    A. ask him to look you in the eye   B. talk to him about sports
    C. tell him he is being very rude   D. change your tone of voice

23.____

24. As a supervisor, you may find it necessary to conduct meetings with your subordinates.
Of the following, which would be MOST helpful in assuring that a meeting accomplishes the purpose for which it was called?
    A. Give notice of the conclusions you would like to reach at the start of the meeting.
    B. Delay the start of the meeting until everyone is present.
    C. Write down points to be discussed in proper sequence.
    D. Make sure everyone is clear on whatever conclusions have been reached and on what must be done after the meeting.

24.____

25. Every supervisor will occasionally be called upon to deliver a reprimand to a subordinate. If done properly, this can greatly help an employee improve his performance.
Which one of the following is NOT a good practice to follow when giving a reprimand?
    A. Maintain your composure and temper
    B. Reprimand a subordinate in the presence of other employees so they can learn the same lesson
    C. Try to understand why the employee was not able to perform satisfactorily
    D. Let your knowledge of the man involved determine the exact nature of the reprimand

25.____

KEY (CORRECT ANSWERS)

1.	C		11.	A
2.	B		12.	A
3.	D		13.	B
4.	B		14.	C
5.	D		15.	A
6.	C		16.	D
7.	C		17.	C
8.	B		18.	C
9.	C		19.	B
10.	C		20.	C

21.	B
22.	B
23.	D
24.	D
25.	B

TEST 2

DIRECTIONS: Each question or incomplete statement is followed by several suggested answers or completions. Select the one that BEST answers the question or completes the statement. *PRINT THE LETTER OF THE CORRECT ANSWER IN THE SPACE AT THE RIGHT.*

1. Usually one thinks of communication as a single step, essentially that of transmitting an idea.
   Actually, however, this is only part of a total process, the FIRST step of which should be
   A. the prompt dissemination of the idea to those who may be affected by it
   B. motivating those affected to take the required action
   C. clarifying the idea in one's own mind
   D. deciding to whom the idea is to be communicated

   1.____

2. Research studies on patterns of informal communication have concluded that most individuals in a group tend to be passive recipients of news, while a few make it their business to spread it around in an organization.
   With this conclusion in mind, it would be MOST correct for the supervisor to attempt to identify these few individuals and
   A. give them the complete facts on important matters in advance of others
   B. inform the other subordinates of the identity of these few individuals so that their influence may be minimized
   C. keep them straight on the facts on important matters
   D. warn them to cease passing along any information to others

   2.____

3. The one of the following which is the PRINCIPAL advantage of making an oral report is that it
   A. affords an immediate opportunity for two-way communication between the subordinate and superior
   B. is an easy method for the superior to use in transmitting information to others of equal rank
   C. saves the time of all concerned
   D. permits more precise pinpointing of praise or blame by means of follow-up questions by the superior

   3.____

4. An agency may sometimes undertake a public relations program of a defensive nature.
   With reference to the use of defensive public relations, it would be MOST correct to state that it
   A. is bound to be ineffective since defensive statements, even though supported by factual data, can never hope to even partly overcome the effects of prior unfavorable attacks
   B. proves that the agency has failed to establish good relationships with newspapers, radio stations, or other means of publicity

   4.____

37

C. shows that the upper echelons of the agency have failed to develop sound public relations procedures and techniques

D. is sometimes required to aid morale by protecting the agency from unjustified criticism and misunderstanding of policies or procedures

5. Of the following factors which contribute to possible undesirable public attitudes towards an agency, the one which is MOST susceptible to being changed by the efforts of the individual employee in an organization is that
    A. enforcement of unpopular regulations as offended many individuals
    B. the organization itself has an unsatisfactory reputation
    C. the public is not interested in agency matters
    D. there are many errors in judgment committed by individual subordinates

5.____

6. It is not enough for an agency's services to be of a high quality; attention must also be given to the acceptability of these services to the general public.
This statement is GENERALLY
    A. *false*; a superior quality of service automatically wins public support
    B. *true*; the agency cannot generally progress beyond the understanding and support of the public
    C. *false*; the acceptance by the public of agency services determines their quality
    D. *true*; the agency is generally unable to engage in any effective enforcement activity without public support

6.____

7. Sustained agency participation in a program sponsored by a community organization is MOST justified when
    A. the achievement of agency objectives in some area depends partly on the activity of this organization
    B. the community organization is attempting to widen the base of participation in all community affairs
    C. the agency is uncertain as to what the community wants
    D. the agency is uncertain as to what the community wants

7.____

8. Of the following, the LEAST likely way in which a records system may serve a supervisor is in
    A. developing a sympathetic and cooperative public attitude toward the agency
    B. improving the quality of supervision by permitting a check on the accomplishment of subordinates
    C. permit a precise prediction of the exact incidences in specific categories for the following year
    D. helping to take the guesswork out of the distribution of the agency

8.____

9.   Assuming that the *grapevine* in any organization is virtually indestructible, the one of the following which it is MOST important for management to understand is:

     A. What is being spread by means of the *grapevine* and the reason for spreading it

     B. What is being spread by means of the *grapevine* and how it is being spread

     C. Who is involved in spreading the information that is on the *grapevine*

     D. Why those who are involved in spreading the information are doing so

9.____

10.   When the supervisor writes a report concerning an investigation to which he has been assigned, it should be LEAST intended to provide

     A. a permanent official record of relevant information gathered

     B. a summary of case findings limited to facts which tend to indicate the guilt of a suspect

     C. a statement of the facts on which higher authorities may base a corrective or disciplinary action

     D. other investigators with information so that they may continue with other phases of the investigation

10.____

11.   In survey work, questionnaires rather than interviews are sometimes used. The one of the following which is a DISADVANTAGE of the questionnaire method as compared with the interview is the

     A. difficulty of accurately interpreting the results

     B. problem of maintaining anonymity of the participant

     C. fact that it is relatively uneconomical

     D. requirement of special training for the distribution of questionnaires

11.____

12.   in his contacts with the public, an employee should attempt to create a good climate of support for his agency.
This statement is GENERALLY

     A. *false*; such attempts are clearly beyond the scope of his responsibility

     B. *true*; employees of an agency who come in contact with the public have the opportunity to affect public relations

     C. *false*; such activity should be restricted to supervisors trained in public relations techniques

     D. *true*; the future expansion of the agency depends to a great extent on continued public support of the agency

12.____

13.   The repeated use by a supervisor of a call for volunteers to get a job done is objectionable MAINLY because it

     A. may create a feeling of animosity between the volunteers and the non-volunteers

     B. may indicate that the supervisor is avoiding responsibility for making assignments which will be most productive

     C. is an indication that the supervisor is not familiar with the individual capabilities of his men

     D. is unfair to men who, for valid reasons, do not, or cannot volunteer

13.____

14. Of the following statements concerning subordinates' expressions to a
    supervisor of their opinions and feelings concerning work situations, the one
    which is MOST correct is that
    A. by listening and responding to such expressions the supervisor
       encourages the development of complaints
    B. the lack of such expressions should indicate to the supervisor that there is
       a high level of job satisfaction
    C. the more the supervisor listens to and responds to such expressions, the
       more he demonstrates lack of supervisory ability
    D. by listening and responding to such expressions, the supervisor will
       enable many subordinates to understand and solve their own problems
       on the job

14.____

15. In attempting to motivate employees, rewards are considered preferable to
    punishment PRIMARILY because
    A. punishment seldom has any effect on human behavior
    B. punishment usually results in decreased production
    C. supervisors find it difficult to punish
    D. rewards are more likely to result in willing cooperation

15.____

16. In an attempt to combat the low morale in his organization, a high level
    supervisor publicized an *open-door policy* to allow employees who wished to
    do so to come to him with their complaints.
    Which of the following is LEAST likely to account for the fact that no employee
    came in with a complaint?
    A. Employees are generally reluctant to go over the heads of their
       immediate supervisor.
    B. The employees did not feel that management would help them.
    C. The low morale was not due to complaints associated with the job.
    D. The employees felt that they had more to lose than to gain.

16.____

17. It is MOST desirable to use written instructions rather than oral instructions for
    a particular job when
    A. a mistake on the job will not be serious
    B. the job can be completed in a short time
    C. there is no need to explain the job minutely
    D. the job involves many details

17.____

18. If you receive a telephone call regarding a matter which your office does not
    handle, you should FIRST
    A. give the caller the telephone number of the proper office so that he can
       dial again
    B. offer to transfer the caller to the proper office
    C. suggest that the caller re-dial since he probably dialed incorrectly
    D. tell the caller he has reached the wrong office and then hang up

18.____

5 (#2)

19. When you answer the telephone, the MOST important reason for identifying
yourself and your organization is to
    A. give the caller time to collect his or her thoughts
    B. impress the caller with your courtesy
    C. inform the caller that he or she has reached the right number
    D. set a business-like tone at the beginning of the conversation

19._____

20. As soon as you pick up the phone, a very angry caller begins immediately to
complain about city agencies and *red tape*. He says that he has been shifted
to two or three different offices. It turs out that he is seeking information which
is not immediately available to you. You believe, you know, however, where it
can be found.
Which of the following actions is the BEST one for you to take?
    A. To eliminate all confusion, suggest that the caller write the agency stating
explicitly what he wants.
    B. Apologize by telling the caller how busy city agencies now are, but also
tell him directly that you do not have the information he needs.
    C. Ask for the caller's telephone number and assure him you will call back
after you have checked further.
    D. Give the caller the name and telephone number of the person who might
be able to help, but explain that you are not positive he will get results/

20._____

21. Which of the following approaches usually provides the BEST communication
in the objectives and values of a new program which is to be introduced?
    A. A general written description of the program by the program manager for
review by those who share responsibility
    B. An effective verbal presentation by the program manager to those
affected
    C. Development of the plan and operational approach in carrying out the
program by the program manager assisted by his key subordinates
    D. Development of the plan by the program manager's supervisor

21._____

22. What is the BEST approach for introducing change?
A
    A. combination of written and also verbal communication to all personnel
affected by the change
    B. general bulletin to all personnel
    C. meeting pointing out all the values of the new approach
    D. written directive to key personnel

22._____

23. Of the following, committees are BEST used for
    A. advising the head of the organization
    B. improving functional work
    C. making executive decisions
    D. making specific planning decisions

23._____

41

24. An effective discussion leader is one who
    A. announces the problem and his preconceived solution at the start of the discussion
    B. guides and directs the discussion according to pre-arranged outline
    C. interrupts or corrects confused participants to save time
    D. permits anyone to say anything at any time

24.____

25. The human relations movement in management theory is basically concerned with
    A. counteracting employee unrest
    B. eliminating the *time and motion* man
    C. interrelationships among individuals in organizations
    D. the psychology of the worker

25.____

_____

KEY (CORRECT ANSWERS)

1.	C		11.	A
2.	C		12.	B
3.	A		13.	B
4.	D		14.	D
5.	D		15.	D
6.	B		16.	C
7.	A		17.	D
8.	C		18.	B
9.	A		19.	C
10.	B		20.	C

21.	C
22.	A
23.	A
24.	B
25.	C

_____

EXAMINATION SECTION
TEST 1

DIRECTIONS: Each question or incomplete statement is followed by several suggested answers or completions. Select the one that BEST answers the question or completes the statement. *PRINT THE LETTER OF THE CORRECT ANSWER IN THE SPACE AT THE RIGHT.*

1.   The model of public relations practice MÓST commonly used by government agencies is the _____ model.

    A.   press agentry/publicity   B.   public information
    C.   two-way asymmetric   D.   two-way symmetric

1._____

2.   Each of the following is one of the four primary areas of government-related public relations practice EXCEPT

    A.   politics
    B.   special interests inside government
    C.   lobbying
    D.   public affairs

2._____

3.   Which of the following statements is considered to be one of the learning principles associated with consumer behaviors?

    A.   It is easier to recall an appeal than to recognize it.
    B.   Appeals made in exhaustive, momentary bursts of information are most effective.
    C.   Unique messages are remembered more completely than others.
    D.   Unpleasant appeals are usually not learned as well as pleasant ones.

3._____

4.   Which phase of the diffusion cycle of persuasive information would occur FIRST?

    A.   Information   B.   Adoption
    C.   Reinforcement   D.   Awareness

4._____

5.   Which of the following is a guideline associated with researching public relations campaigns associated with television or radio broadcasting?

    A.   Design surveys to include primarily open-ended questions
    B.   Attempt to cover the largest area possible
    C.   Collect information by telephone or face-to-face interviews rather than by mail
    D.   Gather information about subject's friends and family members, to conserve time

5._____

6.   In which persuasive strategy is the cost-effectiveness of message repetition MOST problematic?

    A.   Personality appeal   B.   Cognitive
    C.   Stimulus-response   D.   Motivational

6._____

7.   Which of the following is NOT one of the basic ideas behind the effort to influence public opinion?

    A.   Reliability is difficult to assess
    B.   Words, rather than events, are most likely to affect opinion
    C.   Demands for action are a usual response
    D.   Self-interest figures heavily into public involvement

7._____

8. _____ is categorized specifically as a *self-esteem* need that should be considered by the formers of a message.

    A. Knowledge   B. Acceptance
    C. Intellectual curiosity   D. Peace

8.____

9. Which of the following is NOT one of the personal characteristics considered necessary for a public relations practitioner?

    A. Intuition
    B. Specialized cultural background
    C. Training in the social sciences
    D. Objectivity

9.____

10. According to the basic principles of public relations, _____ is the sole criterion by which a public relations professional should be measured.

    A. versatility   B. objectivity
    C. ethical performance   D. demonstrated influence

10.____

11. Which method for determining client charges for public relations services is considered to be the RISKIEST?

    A. Hourly fee
    B. Fee for services and out-of-pocket expenses
    C. Fixed fee
    D. Retainer

11.____

12. According to the conditional probability theory of message receptiveness, the _____ public is among the secondary, rather than primary, group to target with a message.

    A. aware   B. active
    C. latent   D. latent/aware

12.____

13. The Public Relations Society of America's Code of Professional Standards defines political public relations as relating to each of the following EXCEPT the counseling of

    A. candidates or political organizations
    B. clients in connection with the client's relationship with government, with the purpose of influencing legislation
    C. media personnel who want to learn more about a candidate or political organization's record
    D. holders of public office

13.____

14. Which of the following is considered by public relations businesses to be a chargeable expense?

    A. Meetings with clients to prepare account material
    B. Maintaining contacts with media representatives
    C. Meetings with staff and other group conferences related to public relations business
    D. Preparation of materials for potential clients

14.____

15. Of the steps in a problem-oriented public relations campaign listed below, which would occur FIRST?   15.____

    A. Determine communications strategy
    B. Evaluation of problem's impact
    C. Development of organizational strategy
    D. Deciding upon tactics

16. Which function of a public relations practitioner involves analyzing problems and opportunities, as well as assigning responsibilities to appropriate personnel?   16.____

    A. Programming   B. Relationships
    C. Research and evaluation   D. Production

17. Which of the following is an advantage associated with the use of television as a medium for public relations communication?   17.____

    A. Good product identification
    B. Almost unlimited time allotment
    C. The creation of opportunities for consumer referral
    D. Low production costs

18. Which persuasive strategy is designed specifically for *outer-directed* people?   18.____

    A. Personality appeal   B. Social appeal
    C. Stimulus-response   D. Cognitive

19. The _____ model of public relations practice is characterized by an attempt to persuade the public to adopt the organization's point-of-view,   19.____

    A. press agentry/publicity   B. public information
    C. two-way asymmetric   D. two-way symmetric

20. Which of the following is one of the *laws* of public opinion?   20.____

    A. Opinion is basically determined by self-interest.
    B. Generally, public opinion is useful for the anticipation of emergencies.
    C. Opinion is usually sustainable through repetitive appeals.
    D. Generally, opinion is not sensitive to important events

21. In terms of psychographic research, which of the following personality types would be considered *outer-directed?*   21.____

    A. Sustainers   B. Achievers
    C. Experimentals   D. Survivors

22. Which of the following is a disadvantage associated with the use of radio as a medium for public relations communication?   22.____

    A. Time restrictions
    B. Neglect of local markets
    C. Relatively high production costs
    D. Difficulty in altering copy

23. Which of the following statements is NOT one of the basic principles of public relations practice?   23.____

    A. Public relations is primarily a service-oriented profession.
    B. Practitioners depend heavily on scientific public opinion research.
    C. Public relations is concerned not so much with reality as with the public's perception of reality.
    D. Practitioners depend largely on theories and practices of the social sciences.

24. The communication theory which claims that the stability of a society is dependent upon its organization is   24.____

    A. symbolic interactionism   B. structural functionalism
    C. sociocultural paradigm   D. social conflict

25. Which of the following types of measurements would be used to determine the ethical dimensions of a message?   25.____

    A. Powerful-weak   B. Biased-unbiased
    C. Easy-difficult   D. Active-passive

KEY (CORRECT ANSWERS)

1.	B		11.	C
2.	B		12.	B
3.	C		13.	C
4.	D		14.	A
5.	C		15.	B
6.	C		16.	A
7.	B		17.	A
8.	A		18.	A
9.	B		19.	C
10.	C		20.	A

21.	B
22.	A
23.	C
24.	B
25.	B

TEST 2

DIRECTIONS: Each question or incomplete statement is followed by several suggested answers or completions. Select the one that BEST answers the question or completes the statement. *PRINT THE LETTER OF THE CORRECT ANSWER IN THE SPACE AT THE RIGHT.*

1. A typical public relations practitioner spends MOST of his/her professional time with   1.____

   A. lobbying
   B. media contacts/press conferences
   C. radio/television appearances
   D. speechmaking

2. Which of the following is an element of off-premise community relations, as practiced by the administration of an organization?   2.____

   A. Care for the handicapped and aged
   B. Open houses
   C. Offering free consultations
   D. Community bulletin boards

3. Each of the following is an explanation for the typically large budgets associated with the production of an annual report EXCEPT   3.____

   A. that it is the primary means by which most organizations communicate with the public
   B. high deadline pressures
   C. increasing regulation by the Securities and Exchange Commission
   D. that few other public relations methods practiced by the organization require much funding

4. What is the term for a speech written so that several speakers can deliver it to different audiences with only minor variations?   4.____

   A. Semantic   B. Basic   C. Pattern   D. Quota

5. Which of the following is NOT a reason for using the *inverted pyramid* style when writing public relations news releases?   5.____

   A. Good for hurried readers
   B. Will draw attention in opening lines
   C. Gives writer more room to present an idea or event
   D. Can usually be edited or cut without much loss of important information

6. Which of the following is NOT an objective of government information efforts?   6.____

   A. Explain agency techniques in a way that invites input from citizens
   B. Provide citizen feedback to government administrators
   C. Implement changes in the policies of government agencies, aligning with public opinion
   D. Communicate the work of government agencies

7. The model of public relations practice MOST commonly used by highly-regulated busi-   7.____
ness, such as the telephone industry, is the _____ model.

   A. press agentry/publicity   B. public information
   C. two-way asymmetric   D. two-way symmetric

8. Which of the following is an advantage associated with the use of magazines as media   8.____
for public relations communication?

   A. Domination of local markets
   B. Immediacy of message
   C. Nonselective targeting of audience
   D. Access to affluent consumers

9. Which persuasive strategy is designed specifically for people who have no negative pre-   9.____
conceptions about the target behavior?

   A. Personality appeal   B. Social appeal
   C. Motivational   D. Cognitive

10. The pursuit of management objectives through supervision, delegation of authority, and   10.____
work assignments is called the _____ function.

   A. line   B. transfer
   C. staff   D. institutional

11. Which of the following is NOT usually considered part of the necessary contents of inter-   11.____
nal publications?

   A. News stories   B. Employee opinion forum
   C. Feature stories   D. Items of record

12. In communications theory, the person or group that receives a message is known as the   12.____

   A. decoder   B. gatekeeper
   C. encoder   D. planter

13. When scheduling the preparation of public service announcements, APPROXIMATELY   13.____
how much time should be set aside to allow for the choice of a cause or topic?
_____ hours.

   A. 1-2   B. 2-4   C. 4-12   D. 8-16

14. Which of the following is NOT one of the *laws* of public opinion?   14.____

   A. People have more opinions with respect to goals than with respect to the means by
      which to achieve them.
   B. Public opinion is based more on information than desire.
   C. When opinion is not solidly structured, an accomplished fact tends to shift opinion
      in the accepted direction.
   D. Opinion is primarily reactive rather than proactive.

15. When a public relations practitioner selects opinion leaders to be interviewed, in order to   15.____
insure the success of a campaign, this is known as _____ sampling,

   A. probability   B. internal
   C. quota   D. purposive

16. Which of the following is considered by public relations businesses to be a noncharge-able expense?   16.____

    A.   Preparation of visual materials used in presentations
    B.   Off-hours time spent with client personnel on client matters
    C.   Professional development activities such as seminars
    D.   Photographic assignments

17. Which of the following is NOT considered one of the ethical guidelines for people working in political public relations?   17.____
Members shall not

    A.   distribute advertising or publicity information which in unlabeled as to its source
    B.   make gifts to influence decisions of voters or legislators
    C.   engage in the inherently biased practice of partisan advocacy
    D.   through information known to be misleading, intentionally injure the public reputa-tion of the opposing candidate

18. A publicist who delivers new releases to media offices and urges their use is known as a(n)   18.____

    A.   planter   B.   encoder
    C.   gatekeeper   D.   booker

19. According to the conditional probability theory of message receptiveness, the most cost-effective for message distribution is a(n) _____ public characterized by _____ behav-iors.   19.____

    A.   latent/aware; constrained
    B.   latent; routine
    C.   active; problem-facing
    D.   inactive; fatalistic

20. The communication theory which claims that the media's constructs of reality ultimately result in a society's individual and collective creations of reality is called   20.____

    A.   symbolic interactionism
    B.   social conflict
    C.   evolutionary perspective
    D.   psychodynamic model

21. Which of the following is an advantage associated with the use of direct mailing as a medium for public relations communication?   21.____

    A.   Relaxed regulation of content
    B.   Inexpensive
    C.   Selectivity of target audience
    D.   Consistency of mailing lists

22. Each of the following elements in a persuasive message is considered essential to pro-voking a response EXCEPT   22.____

    A.   familiarity and trust   B.   spirited challenge
    C.   identification   D.   suggestion of action

23. Which function of a public relations practitioner requires background knowledge of art, layout, and photography?   23.____

    A. Programming   B. Information
    C. Research and evaluation   D. Production

24. In researching public relations campaigns associated with television or radio broadcasting, what is generally considered to be the upper limit for the cross-section of the public necessary to provide an adequate information sample?   24.____

    A. 100   B. 500   C. 1,000   D. 5,000

25. Of the steps in scheduling an annual report listed below, which would occur FIRST?   25.____

    A. Producing copy
    B. Assigning work
    C. Clearing material recommendations
    D. Production

KEY (CORRECT ANSWERS)

1.	B		11.	B
2.	A		12.	A
3.	D		13.	C
4.	C		14.	D
5.	C		15.	B
6.	C		16.	C
7.	D		17.	C
8.	D		18.	A
9.	D		19.	A
10.	A		20.	A

21.	C
22.	B
23.	D
24.	C
25.	B

READING COMPREHENSION
UNDERSTANDING AND INTERPRETING WRITTEN MATERIAL
EXAMINATION SECTION
TEST 1

DIRECTIONS: Each question or incomplete statement is followed by several suggested
answers or completions. Select the one that BEST answers the question or
completes the statement. *PRINT THE LETTER OF THE CORRECT ANSWER
IN THE SPACE AT THE RIGHT.*

1.   The National Assessment of Educational Progress recently released the results   1.____
of the first statistically valid national sampling of young adult reading skills in
the United States. According to the survey, ninety-five percent of United States
young adults (aged 21-25) can read at a fourth-grade level or better. This
means they can read well enough to apply for a job, understand a movie guide
or join the Army. This is a higher literacy rate than the eighty to eighty-five
percent usually estimated for all adults. The study also found that ninety-nine
percent can write their names, eighty percent can read a map or write a check
for a bill, seventy percent can understand an appliance warranty or write a
letter about a billing error, twenty-five percent can calculate the amount of a tip
correctly, and fewer than ten percent can correctly figure the cost of a catalog
or understand a complex bus schedule.
Which statement about the study is BEST supported by the above passage?
   A. United States literacy rates among young adults are at an all-time high.
   B. Forty percent of young people in the United States cannot write a letter
      about a billing error.
   C. Twenty percent of United States teenagers cannot read a map,
   D. More than ninety percent of United States young adults cannot correctly
      calculate the cost of a catalog order.

2.   It is now widely recognized that salaries, benefits, and working conditions have   2.____
more of an impact on job satisfaction than on motivation. If they aren't
satisfactory, work performance and morale will suffer. But even when they are
high, employees will not necessarily be motivated to work well. For example,
THE WALL STREET JOURNAL recently reported that as many as forty or fifty
percent of newly hired Wall Street lawyers (whose salaries start at upwards of
$50,000) quit within the first three years, citing long hours, pressures, and
monotony as the prime offenders. It seems there's just not enough of an
intellectual challenge in their jobs. An up and coming money-market executive
concluded: *Whether it was $1 million or $100 million, the procedure was the
same. Except for the tension, a baboon could do my job.* When money and
benefits are adequate, the most important additional determinants of job
satisfaction are: more responsibility, a sense of achievement, recognition, and
a chance to advance. All of these factors have a more significant influence on
employee motivation and performance. As a footnote, several studies have
found that the absence of these non-monetary factors can lead to serious
stress-related illnesses.

Which statement is BEST supported by the above passage?
  A. A worker's motivation to perform well is most affected by salaries, benefits, and working conditions.
  B. Low pay can lead to high levels of job stress.
  C. Work performance will suffer if workers feel they are not paid well.
  D. After satisfaction with pay and benefits, the next most important factor is more responsibility.

3. The establishment of joint labor-management production committees occurred in the United States during World War I and again during World War II. Their use was greatly encouraged by the National War Labor Board in World War I and the War Production Board in 1942. Because of the war, labor-management cooperation was especially desired to produce enough goods for the war effort, to reduce conflict, and to control inflation. The committees focused on how to achieve greater efficiency, and consulted on health and safety, training, absenteeism, and people issues in general. During the second world war, there were approximately five thousand labor-management committees in factories, affecting over six million workers. While research has found that only a few hundred committees made significant contributions to productivity, there were additional benefits in many cases. It became obvious to many that workers had ideas to contribute to the running of the organization, and that efficient enterprises could become even more so. Labor-management cooperation was also extended to industries that had never experienced it before. Directly after each war, however, few United States labor-management committees were in operation.
Which statement is BEST supported by the above passage?
  A. The majority of United States labor-management committees during the second world war accomplished little.
  B. A major goal of United States labor-management committees during the first and second world wars was to increase productivity.
  C. There were more United States labor-management committees during the second world war than during the first world war.
  D. There are few United States labor-management committees in operation today.

3.____

4. Studies have found that stress levels among employees who have a great deal of customer contact or a great deal of contact with the public can be very high. There are many reasons for this. Sometimes stress results when the employee is caught in the middle—an organization wants things done one way, but the customer wants them done another way. The situation becomes even worse for the employee's stress levels when he or she knows was to more effectively provide the service, but isn't allowed to, by the organization. An example is the bank teller who is required to ask a customer for two forms of identification before he or she can cash a check, even though the teller knows the customer well. If organizational mishaps occur or if there are problems with job design, the employee may be powerless to satisfy the customer, and also powerless to protect himself or herself from the customer's wrath. An example of this is the waitress who is forced to serve poorly prepared food. Studies have also found,

4.____

however, that if the organization and the employee design the positions and the service encounter well, and encourage the use of effective stress management techniques, stress can be reduced to levels that are well below average.
Which statement is BEST supported by the above passage?
    A. It is likely that knowledgeable employees will experience greater levels of job-related stress.
    B. The highest levels of occupational stress are found among those employees who have a great deal of customer contact.
    C. Organizations can contribute to the stress levels of their employees by poorly designing customer contact situations.
    D. Stress levels are generally higher in banks and restaurants.

5. It is estimated that approximately half of the United States population suffers from varying degrees of adrenal malfunction. When under stress for long periods of time, the adrenals produce extra cortisol and norepinephrine. By producing more hormones than they were designed to comfortably manufacture and secrete, the adrenals can *burn out* over time and then decrease their secretion. When this happens, the body loses its capacity to cope with stress, and the individual becomes sicker more easily and for longer periods of time. A result of adrenal malfunction may be a diminished output of cortisol. Symptoms of diminished cortisol output include any of the following: craving substances that will temporarily raise serum glucose levels such as caffeine, sweets, soda, juice, or tobacco; becoming dizzy when standing up too quickly; irritability; headaches; and erratic energy levels. Since cortisol is an anti-inflammatory hormone, a decreased output over extended periods of time can make one prone to inflammatory disease such ass arthritis, bursitis, colitis, and allergies. (Many food and pollen allergies disappear when adrenal function is restored to normal.) The patient will have no reserve energy, and infections can spread quickly. Excessive cortisol production, on the other hand, can decrease immunity, leading to frequent and prolonged illnesses.
Which statement is BEST supported by the above passage?
    A. Those who suffer from adrenal malfunction are most likely to be prone to inflammatory diseases such as arthritis and allergies.
    B. The majority of Americans suffer from varying degrees of adrenal malfunction.
    C. It is better for the health of the adrenals to drink juice instead of soda.
    D. Too much cortisol can inhibit the body's ability to resist disease.

6. Psychologist B.F. Skinner pointed out long ago that gambling is reinforced either by design or accidentally, by what he called a variable ratio schedule. A slot machine, for example, is cleverly designed to provide a payoff after it has been played a variable number of times. Although the person who plays it and wins while playing receives a great deal of monetary reinforcement, over the long run the machine will take in much more money than it pays out. Research on both animals and humans has consistently found that such variable reward schedules maintain a very high rate of repeat behavior, and that this behavior is particularly resistant to extinction.

5.____

6.____

Which statement is BEST supported by the above passage?
- A. Gambling, because it is reinforced by the variable ratio schedule, is more difficult to eliminate than most addictions.
- B. If someone is rewarded or wins consistently, even if it is not that often, he or she is likely to continue that behavior.
- C. Playing slot machines is the safest form of gambling because they are designed so that eventually the player will indeed win.
- D. A cat is likely to come when called if its owner has trained it correctly,

7. Paper entrepreneurialism is an offshoot of scientific management that has become so extreme that it has lost all connection to the actual workplace. It generates profits by cleverly manipulating rules and numbers that only in theory represent real products and real assets. At its worst, paper entrepreneurialism involves very little more than imposing losses on others for the sake of short-term profits. The others may be taxpayers, shareholders who end up indirectly subsidizing other shar holders, consumers, or investors. Paper entrepreneurialism has replaced product entrepreneurialism, is seriously threatening the United States economy, and is hurting our necessary attempts to transform the nation's industrial and productive economic base. An example is the United States company that complained loudly in 1979 that it did not have the $200 million needed to develop a video-cassette recorder, though demand for them had been very high. The company, however, did not hesitate to spend $1.2 billion that same year to buy a mediocre finance company. The video recorder market was handed over to other countries, who did not hesitate to manufacture them.
Which statement is BEST supported by the above passage?
- A. Paper entrepreneurialism involves very little more than imposing losses on others for the sake of short-term profits.
- B. Shareholders are likely to benefit most from paper entrepreneurialism.
- C. Paper entrepreneurialism is hurting the United States economy.
- D. The United States could have made better video-cassette recorders than the Japanese but we ceded the market to them in 1979.

7.____

8. The *prisoner's dilemma* is an almost 40-year-old game-theory model psychologists, biologists, economists, and political scientists use to try to understand the dynamics of competition and cooperation. Participants in the basic version of the experiment are told that they and their *accomplice* have been caught red-handed. Together, their best strategy is to cooperate by remaining silent. If they do this, each will get off with a 30-day sentence. But either person can do better for himself or herself. If you double-cross your partner, you will go scot free while he or she serves ten years. The problem is, if you each betray the other, you will both go to prison for eight years, not thirty days. No matter what your partner chooses, you are logically better off choosing betrayal. Unfortunately, your partner realizes this too, and so the odds are good that you will both get eight years. That's the dilemma. (The length of the prison sentences is always the same for each variation.) Participants at a recent symposium on behavioral economics at Harvard University discussed the many variations on the game that have been used

8.____

over the years. In one standard version, subjects are paired with a supervisor who pays them a dollar for each point they score. Over the long run, both subjects will do best if they cooperate every time. Yet in each round, there is a great temptation to betray the other because no one knows what the other will do. The best overall strategy for this variation was found to be *tit for tat*, doing unto your opponent as he or she has just done unto you. It is a simple strategy, but very effective. The partner can easily recognize it and respond. It is retaliatory enough not to be easily exploited, but forgiving enough to allow a pattern of mutual cooperation to develop.
Which statement is BEST supported by the above passage?
   A. The best strategy for playing *prisoner's dilemma* is to cooperate and remain silent.
   B. If you double-cross your partner, and he or she does not double-cross you, your partner will receive a sentence of eight years.
   C. When playing *prisoner's dilemma*, it is best to double-cross your partner.
   D. If you double-cross your partner, and he or she double-crosses you, you will receive an eight-year sentence.

9. After many years of experience as the vice president and general manager of a large company, I feel that I know what I'm looking for in a good manager. First, the manager has to be comfortable with himself or herself, and not be arrogant or defensive. Secondly, he or she has to have a genuine interest in people. There are some managers who love ideas—and that's fine—but to be a manager, you must love people, and you must make a hobby of understanding them, believing in them and trusting them. Third, I look for a willingness and a facility to manage conflict. Gandhi defined conflict as a way of getting at the truth. Each person brings his or her own grain of truth and the conflict washes away the illusion and fantasy. Finally, a manager has to have a vision, and the ability and charisma to articulate it. A manager should be seen as a little bit crazy. Some eccentricity is an asset. People don't want to follow vanilla leaders. They want to follow chocolate-fudge-ripple leaders.
Which statement is BEST supported by the above passage?
   A. It is very important that a good manager spend time studying people.
   B. It is critical for good managers to love ideas.
   C. Managers should try to minimize or avoid conflict.
   D. Managers should be familiar with people's reactions to different flavors of ice cream.

9.____

10. Most societies maintain a certain set of values and assumptions that make their members feel either good or bad about themselves, and either better or worse than other people. In most developed countries, these values are based on the assumption that we are all free to be what we want to be, and that differences in income, work, and education are a result of our own efforts. This may make us believe that people with more income work that is more skilled, more education, and more power are somehow *better* people. We may view their achievements as proof that they have more intelligence, more motivation, and more initiative than those with lower status. The myth tells us that power, income, and education are freely and equally available to all, and that our

10.____

failure to achieve them is due to our own personal inadequacy. This simply is not the case.

The possessions we own may also seem to point to our real worth as individuals. The more we own, the more worthy of respect we may feel we are. Or, the acquisition of possessions may be a way of trying to fulfill ourselves, to make up for the loss of community and/or purpose. It is a futile pursuit because lost community and purpose can never be compensated for by better cars or fancier houses. And too often, when these things fail to satisfy, we believe it is only because we don't have enough money to buy better quality items, or more items. We feel bad that we haven't been successful enough to get all that we think we need. No matter how much we do have, goods never really satisfy for long. There is always something else to acquire, and true satisfaction eludes many, many of us.

Which statement is BEST supported by the above passage?
- A. The author would agree with the theory of *survival of the fittest*.
- B. The possessions an individual owns are not a proper measure of his or her real worth.
- C. Many countries make a sincere attempt to ensure equal access to quality education for their citizens.
- D. The effect a society's value system has on the lives of its members is greatly exaggerated.

11. *De nihilo nihil* is Latin for *nothing comes from nothing*. In the first century, the Roman poet Persius advised that if anything is to be produced of value, effort must be expended. He also said, *In nihilum nil posse revorti*—anything once produced cannot become nothing again. It is thought that Persius was parodying Lucretius, who expounded the 500-year-old physical theories of Epicurus. *De nihilo nihil* can also be used as a cynical comment, to negatively comment on something that is of poor quality produced by a person of little talent. The implication here is: *What can you expect from such a source?*

Which statement is BEST supported by the above passage?
- A. *In nihilum nil posse revorti* can be interpreted as meaning, *If anything is to be produced of value, then effort must be expended.*
- B. *De nihilo nihil* can be understood in two different ways,
- C. Lucretius was a great physicist.
- D. Persius felt that Epicurus put in little effort while developing his theories.

11._____

12. A Cornell University study has found that less than one percent of the billion pounds of pesticides used in this country annually strike their intended targets. The study found that the pesticides, which are somewhat haphazardly applied to 370 million acres, or about sixteen percent of the nation's total land area, end up polluting the environment and contaminating almost all 200,000 species of plants and animals, including humans. While the effect of indirect contamination on human cancer rates was not estimated, the study found that approximately 45,000 human pesticide poisonings occur annually, including about 3,000 cases admitted to hospitals and approximately 200 fatalities.

12._____

Which statement is BEST supported by the above passage?
- A. It is likely that indirect pesticide contamination affects human health.
- B. Pesticides are applied to over one-quarter of the total United States land area.
- C. If pesticides were applied more carefully, fewer pesticide-resistant strains of pests would develop.
- D. Human cancer rates in this country would drop considerably if pesticide use was cut in half.

13. The new conservative philosophy presents a unified, coherent approach to the world. It offers to explain much of our experience since the turbulent 1960s, and it shows what we've learned since about the dangers of indulgence and permissiveness. But it also warns that the world has become more ruthless, and that as individuals and as a nation, we must struggle for survival. It is necessary to impose responsibility and discipline in order to defeat those forces that threaten us. This lesson is dramatically clear, and can be applied to a wide range of issues.
Which statement is BEST supported by the above passage?
- A. The 1970s were a time of permissiveness and indulgence.
- B. The new conservative philosophy may help in imposing discipline and a sense of responsibility in order to meet the difficult challenges facing this country.
- C. The world faced greater challenges during the second world war than it faces at the present time.
- D. More people identify themselves today as conservative in their political philosophy.

13._____

14. One of the most puzzling questions in management in recent years has been how usually honest, compassionate, intelligent managers can sometimes act in ways that are dishonest, uncaring, and unethical. How could top-level managers at the Manville Corporation, for example, suppress evidence for decades that proved beyond all doubt that asbestos inhalation was killing their own employees? What drove the managers of a Midwest bank to continue to act in a way that threatened to bankrupt the institution, ruin its reputation, and cost thousands of employees and investors their jobs and their savings? It's been estimated that about two out of three of America's five hundred largest corporations have been involved in some form of illegal behavior. There are, of course, some common rationalizations used to justify unethical conduct: believing that the activity is in the organization's or the individual's best interest, believing that the activity is not *really* immoral or illegal, believing that no one will ever know, or believing that the organization will sanction the behavior because it helps the organization. Ambition can distort one's sense of *duty*.
Which statement is BEST supported by the above passage?
- A. Top-level managers of corporations are currently involved in a plan to increase ethical behavior among their employees.
- B. There are many good reasons why a manager may act unethically.
- C. Some managers allow their ambitions to override their sense of ethics,
- D. In order to successfully compete, some organizations may have to indulge in unethical or illegal behavior from time to time.

14._____

15. Some managers and supervisors believe that they are leaders because they occupy positions of responsibility and authority. But leadership is more than holding a position. It is often defined in management literature as *the ability to influence the opinions, attitudes and behaviors of others.* Obviously, there are some managers that would not qualify as leaders, and some leaders that are not *technically* managers. Research has found that many people overrate their own leadership abilities. In one recent study, seventy percent of those surveyed rated themselves in the top quartile in leadership abilities, and only two percent felt they were below average as leaders.

   Which statement is BEST supported by the above passage?
   A. In a recent study, the majority of people surveyed rated themselves in the top twenty-five percent in leadership abilities.
   B. Ninety-eight percent of the people surveyed in a recent study had average or above-average leadership skills.
   C. In order to be a leader, one should hold a management position.
   D. Leadership is best defined as the ability to be liked by those one must lead.

15.____

———————

KEY (CORRECT ANSWERS)

1.	D	6.	B	11.	B
2.	C	7.	C	12.	A
3.	B	8.	D	13.	B
4.	C	9.	A	14.	C
5.	D	10.	B	15.	A

———————

PREPARING WRITTEN MATERIALS

EXAMINATION SECTION
TEST 1

DIRECTIONS: Each question or incomplete statement is followed by several suggested answers or completions. Select the one that BEST answers the question or completes the statement. *PRINT THE LETTER OF THE CORRECT ANSWER IN THE SPACE AT THE RIGHT.*

Questions 1-21.

DIRECTIONS: In each of the following sentences, which were taken from students' transcripts, there may be an error. Indicate the appropriate correction in the space at the right. If the sentence is correct as is, indicate this choice. Unnecessary changes will be considered incorrect.

1. In that building there seemed to be representatives of Teachers College, the Veterans Bureau, and the Businessmen's Association.
   A. Teacher's College
   B. Veterans' Bureau
   C. Businessmens Association
   D. Correct as is

   1.____

2. In his travels, he visited St. Paul, San Francisco, Springfield, Ohio, and Washington, D.C.
   A. Ohio and
   B. Saint Paul
   C. Washington, D.C.
   D. Correct as is

   2.____

3. As a result of their purchasing a controlling interest in the syndicate, it was well-known that the Bureau of Labor Statistics' calculations would be unimportant.
   A. of them purchasing
   B. well known
   C. Statistics
   D. Correct as is

   3.____

4. Walter Scott, Jr.'s, attempt to emulate his father's success was doomed to failure.
   A. Junior's,
   B. Scott's, Jr.
   C. Scott, Jr.'s attempt
   D. Correct as is

   4.____

5. About B.C. 250 the Romans invaded Great Britain, and remains of their highly developed civilization can still be seen.
   A. 250 B.C.
   B. Britain and
   C. highly-developed
   D. Correct as is

   5.____

6. The two boss's sons visited the children's department.
   A. bosses
   B. bosses'
   C. childrens'
   D. Correct as is

   6.____

7. Miss Amex not only approved the report, but also decided that it needed no revision.
   A. report; but
   B. report but
   C. report. But
   D. Correct as is

   7.____

8. Here's brain food in a jiffy—economical, too!　　8.____

   A. economical too!　　　　B. 'brain food'
   C. jiffy-economical　　　　D. Correct as is

9. She said, "He likes the "Gatsby Look" very much."　　9.____

   A. said "He　　　　B. "he
   C. 'Gatsby Look'　　　　D. Correct as is

10. We anticipate that we will be able to visit them briefly in Los Angeles on Wednesday after a five-day visit.　　10.____

   A. Wednes-　　　　B. 5 day
   C. five day　　　　D. Correct as is

11. She passed all her tests, and, she now has a good position.　　11.____

   A. tests, and she　　　　B. past
   C. tests;　　　　D. Correct as is

12. The billing clerk said, "I will send the bill today"; however, that was a week ago, and it hasn't arrived yet!　　12.____

   A. today;"　　　　B. today,"
   C. ago and　　　　D. Correct as is

13. "She types at more-than-average speed," Miss Smith said, "but I feel that it is a result of marvelous concentration and self control on her part."　　13.____

   A. more than average　　　　B. "But
   C. self-control　　　　D. Correct as is

14. The state of Alaska, the largest state in the union, is also the northernmost state.　　14.____

   A. Union　　　　B. Northernmost State
   C. State of Alaska　　　　D. Correct as is

15. The memoirs of Ex-President Nixon, according to figures, sold more copies than <u>Six Crises</u>, the book he wrote in the 60's.　　15.____

   A. Six Crises　　　　B. ex-President
   C. 60s　　　　D. Correct as is

16. "There are three principal elements, determining the hazard of buildings: the contents hazard, the fire resistance of the structure, and the character of the interior finish," concluded the speaker.
The one of the following statements that is MOST acceptable is that, in the above passage,　　16.____

   A. the comma following the word *elements* is incorrect
   B. the colon following the word *buildings* is incorrect
   C. the comma following the word *finish* is incorrect
   D. there is no error in the punctuation of the sentence

17. He spoke on his favorite topic, "Why We Will Win." (How could I stop him?)　　17.____

   A. Win".　　　　B. him?).
   C. him)?　　　　D. Correct as is

18. "All any insurance policy is, is a contract for services," said my insurance agent, Mr. Newton. 18.____

    A. Insurance Policy   B. Insurance Agent
    C. policy is is a   D. Correct as is

19. Inasmuch as the price list has now been up dated, we should send it to the printer. 19.____

    A. In as much   B. updated
    C. pricelist   D. Correct as is

20. We feel that "Our know-how" is responsible for the improvement in technical developments. 20.____

    A. "our   B. know how
    C. that,   D. Correct as is

21. Did Cortez conquer the Incas? the Aztecs? the South American Indians? 21.____

    A. Incas, the Aztecs, the South American Indians?
    B. Incas; the Aztecs; the South American Indians?
    C. south American Indians?
    D. Correct as is

22. Which one of the following forms for the typed name of the dictator in the closing lines of a letter is generally MOST acceptable in the United States? 22.____

    A. (Dr.) James F. Farley
    B. Dr. James F. Farley
    C. Mr. James F. Farley, Ph.D.
    D. James F. Farley

23. The plural of 23.____

    A. turkey is turkies
    B. cargo is cargoes
    C. bankruptcy is bankruptcys
    D. son-in-law is son-in-laws

24. The abbreviation *viz.* means MOST NEARLY 24.____

    A. namely   B. for example
    C. the following   D. see

25. In the sentence, *A man in a light-gray suit waited thirty-five minutes in the ante-room for the all-important document,* the word IMPROPERLY hyphenated is 25.____

    A. light-gray   B. thirty-five
    C. ante-room   D. all-important

KEY (CORRECT ANSWERS)

1.	D		11.	A
2.	C		12.	D
3.	B		13.	D
4.	D		14.	A
5.	A		15.	B
6.	B		16.	A
7.	B		17.	D
8.	D		18.	D
9.	C		19.	B
10.	C		20.	A

21.	D
22.	D
23.	B
24.	A
25.	C

TEST 2

Questions 1-10.

DIRECTIONS: In each of the following groups of four sentences, one sentence contains an error in sentence structure, grammar, usage, diction, or punctuation. Indicate the INCORRECT sentence.

1. A. The lecture finished, the audience began asking questions.   1.____
    B. Any man who could accomplish that task the world would regard as a hero.
    C. Our respect and admiration are mutual.
    D. George did like his mother told him, despite the importunities of his playmates.

2. A. I cannot but help admiring you for your dedication to your job.   2.____
    B. Because they had insisted upon showing us films of their travels, we have lost many friends whom we once cherished.
    C. I am constrained to admit that your remarks made me feel bad.
    D. My brother having been notified of his acceptance by the university of his choice, my father immediately made plans for a vacation.

3. A. In no other country is freedom of speech and assembly so jealously guarded.   3.____
    B. Being a beatnik, he felt that it would be a betrayal of his cause to wear shoes and socks at the same time.
    C. Riding over the Brooklyn Bridge gave us an opportunity to see the Manhattan skyline.
    D. In 1961, flaunting SEATO, the North Vietnamese crossed the line of demarcation.

4. A. I have enjoyed the study of the Spanish language not only because of its beauty   4.____
        and the opportunity it offers to understand the Hispanic culture but also to make use of it in the business associations I have in South America.
    B. The opinions he expressed were decidedly different from those he had held in his youth.
    C. Had he actually studied, he certainly would have passed.
    D. A supervisor should be patient, tactful, and firm.

5. A. At this point we were faced with only three alternatives: to push on, to remain   5.____
        where we were, or to return to the village.
    B. We had no choice but to forgive so venial a sin.
    C. In their new picture, the Warners are flouting tradition.
    D. Photographs taken revealed that 2.5 square miles had been burned.

6.
    A. He asked whether he might write to his friends.
    B. There are many problems which must be solved before we can be assured of world peace.
    C. Each person with whom I talked expressed his opinion freely.
    D. Holding on to my saddle with all my strength the horse galloped down the road at a terrifying pace.

6.____

7.
    A. After graduating high school, he obtained a position as a runner in Wall Street.
    B. Last night, in a radio address, the President urged us to subscribe to the Red Cross.
    C. In the evening, light spring rain cooled the streets.
    D. "Un-American" is a word which has been used even by those whose sympathies may well have been pro-Nazi.

7.____

8.
    A. It is hard to conceive of their not doing good work.
    B. Who won - you or I?
    C. He having read the speech caused much comment.
    D. Their finishing the work proves that it can be done.

8.____

9.
    A. Our course of study should not be different now than it was five years ago.
    B. I cannot deny myself the pleasure of publicly thanking the mayor for his actions.
    C. The article on "Morale" has appeared in the Times Literary Supplement.
    D. He died of tuberculosis contracted during service with the Allied Forces.

9.____

10.
    A. If it wasn't for a lucky accident, he would still be an office-clerk.
    B. It is evident that teachers need help.
    C. Rolls of postage stamps may be bought at stationery stores.
    D. Addressing machines are used by firms that publish magazines.

10.____

11. The one of the following sentences which contains NO error in usage is:

    A. After the robbers left, the proprietor stood tied in his chair for about two hours before help arrived.
    B. In the cellar I found the watchmans' hat and coat.
    C. The persons living in adjacent apartments stated that they had heard no unusual noises.
    D. Neither a knife or any firearms were found in the room.

11.____

12. The one of the following sentences which contains NO error in usage is:

    A. The policeman lay a firm hand on the suspect's shoulder.
    B. It is true that neither strength nor agility are the most important requirement for a good patrolman.
    C. Good citizens constantly strive to do more than merely comply the restraints imposed by society.
    D. Twenty years is considered a severe sentence for a felony.

12.____

13. Select the sentence containing an adverbial objective.

    A. Concepts can only acquire content when they are connected, however indirectly, with sensible experience.
    B. The cloth was several shades too light to match the skirt which she had discarded.

13.____

C. The Gargantuan Hall of Commons became a tri-daily horror to Kurt, because two youths discerned that he had a beard and courageously told the world about it.
D. Brooding morbidly over the event, Elsie found herself incapable of engaging in normal activity.

14. Select the sentence containing a verb in the subjunctive mood.   14.____

A. Had he known of the new experiments with penicillin dust for the cure of colds, he might have been tempted to try them in his own office.
B. I should be very much honored by your visit.
C. Though he has one of the highest intelligence quotients in his group, he seems far below the average in actual achievement.
D. Long had I known that he would be the man finally selected for such signal honors.

15. Select the sentence containing one (or more) passive perfect participle(s).   15.____

A. Having been apprised of the consequences of his refusal to answer, the witness finally revealed the source of his information.
B. To have been placed in such an uncomfortable position was perhaps unfair to a journalist of his reputation.
C. When deprived of special immunity he had, of course, no alternative but to speak.
D. Having been obdurate until now, he was reluctant to surrender under this final pressure exerted upon him.

16. Select the sentence containing a predicate nominative.   16.____

A. His dying wish, which he expressed almost with his last breath, was to see that justice was done toward his estranged wife.
B. So long as we continue to elect our officials in truly democratic fashion, we shall have the power to preserve our liberties.
C. We could do nothing, at this juncture, but walk the five miles back to camp.
D. There was the spaniel, wet and cold and miserable, waiting silently at the door.

17. Select the sentence containing exactly TWO adverbs.   17.____

A. The gentlemen advanced with exasperating deliberateness, while his lonely partner waited.
B. If you are well, will you come early?
C. I think you have guessed right, though you were rather slow, I must say.
D. The last hundred years have seen more change than a thousand years of the Roman Empire, than a hundred thousand years of the stone age.

Questions 18-24.

DIRECTIONS: Select the choice describing the error in the sentence.

18. If us seniors do not support school functions, who will?   18.____

A. Unnecessary shift in tense
B. Incomplete sentence
C. Improper case of pronoun
D. Lack of parallelism

19. The principal has issued regulations which, in my opinion, I think are too harsh.   19.____

    A. Incorrect punctuation   B. Faulty sentence structure
    C. Misspelling   D. Redundant expression

20. The freshmens' and sophomores' performances equaled those of the juniors and   20.____
seniors.

    A. Ambiguous reference
    B. Incorrect placement of punctuation
    C. Misspelling of past tense
    D. Incomplete comparison

21. Each of them, Anne and her, is an outstanding pianist; I can't tell you which one is best.   21.____

    A. Lack of agreement
    B. Improper degree of comparison
    C. Incorrect case of pronoun
    D. Run-on sentence

22. She wears clothes that are more expensive than my other friends.   22.____

    A. Misuse of *than*   B. Incorrect relative pronoun
    C. Shift in tense   D. Faulty comparison

23. At the very end of the story it implies that the children's father died tragically.   23.____

    A. Misuse of *implies*   B. Indefinite use of pronoun
    C. Incorrect spelling   D. Incorrect possessive

24. At the end of the game both of us, John and me, couldn't scarcely walk because we were   24.____
so tired.

    A. Incorrect punctuation
    B. Run-on sentence
    C. Incorrect case of pronoun
    D. Double negative

Questions 25-30.

DIRECTIONS: Questions 25 through 30 consist of a sentence lacking certain needed punctuation. Pick as your answer the description of punctuation which will CORRECTLY complete the sentence.

25. If you take the time to keep up your daily correspondence you will no doubt be most efficient.   25.____

    A. Comma only after *doubt*
    B. Comma only after *correspondence*
    C. Commas after *correspondence, will,* and *be*
    D. Commas after *if, correspondence,* and *will*

26. Because he did not send the application soon enough he did not receive the up to date   26.____
    copy of the book.

    A. Commas after *application* and *enough*, and quotation marks before *up* and after
       date
    B. Commas after *application* and *enough*, and hyphens between *to* and *date*
    C. Comma after *enough*, and hyphens between *up* and *to* and between *to* and *date*
    D. Comma after *application*, and quotation marks before *up* and after *date*

27. The coordinator requested from the department the following items a letter each week   27.____
    summarizing progress personal forms and completed applications for tests.

    A. Commas after *items* and *completed*
    B. Semi-colon after *items* and *progress*, comma after *forms*
    C. Colon after *items*, commas after *progress* and *forms*
    D. Colon after *items*, commas after *forms* and *applications*

28. The supervisor asked Who will attend the conference next month.   28.____

    A. Comma after *asked*, period after *month*
    B. Period after *asked*, question mark after *month*
    C. Comma after *asked*, quotation marks before *Who*, quotation marks after *month*,
       and question mark after the quotation marks
    D. Comma after *asked*, quotation marks before *Who*, question mark after *month*, and
       quotation marks after the question mark

29. When the statistics are collected, we will forward the results to you as soon as possible. 29.____

    A. Comma after *you*
    B. Commas after *forward* and *you*
    C. Commas after *collected*, *results*, and *you*
    D. Comma after *collected*

30. The ecology of our environment is concerned with mans pollution of the atmosphere.   30.____

    A. Comma after *ecology*
    B. Apostrophe after *n* and before *s* in *mans*
    C. Commas after *ecology* and *environment*
    D. Apostrophe after *s* in *mans*

———————

KEY (CORRECT ANSWERS)

1.	D	16.	A
2.	A	17.	C
3.	D	18.	C
4.	A	19.	D
5.	B	20.	B
6.	D	21.	B
7.	A	22.	D
8.	C	23.	B
9.	A	24.	D
10.	A	25.	B
11.	C	26.	C
12.	D	27.	C
13.	B	28.	D
14.	A	29.	D
15.	A	30.	B

TEST 3

DIRECTIONS: Each question or incorrect statement is followed by several suggested answers or completions. Select the one that BEST answers the question or completes the statement. *PRINT THE LETTER OF THE CORRECT ANSWER IN THE SPACE AT THE RIGHT.*

Questions 1-6.

DIRECTIONS: From the four choices offered in Questions 1 through 6, select the one which is INCORRECT.

1. A. Before we try to extricate ourselves from this struggle in which we are now engaged in, we must be sure that we are not severing ties of honor and duty.
    B. Besides being an outstanding student, he is also a leader in school government and a trophy-winner in school sports.
    C. If the framers of the Constitution were to return to life for a day, their opinion of our amendments would be interesting.
    D. Since there are three m's in the word, it is frequently misspelled.

1.____

2. A. It was a college with an excellance beyond question.
    B. The coach will accompany the winners, whomever they may be.
    C. The dean, together with some other faculty members, is planning a conference.
    D. The jury are arguing among themselves.

2.____

3. A. This box is less nearly square than that one.
    B. Wagner is many persons' choice as the world's greatest composer.
    C. The habits of Copperheads are different from Diamond Backs.
    D. The teacher maintains that the child was insolent.

3.____

4. A. There was a time when the Far North was unknown territory. Now American soldiers manning radar stations there wave to Boeing jet planes zooming by overhead.
    B. Exodus, the psalms, and Deuteronomy are all books of the Old Testament.
    C. Linda identified her china dishes by marking their bottoms with india ink.
    D. Harry S. Truman, former president of the United States, served as a captain in the American army during World War I.

4.____

5. A. The sequel of their marriage was a divorce.
    B. We bought our car secondhand.
    C. His whereabouts is unknown.
    D. Jones offered to use his own car, providing the company would pay for gasoline, oil, and repairs.

5.____

6. A. I read Golding's "Lord of the Flies".
    B. The orator at the civil rights rally thrilled the audience when he said, "I quote Robert Burns's line, 'A man's a man for a' that.'"
    C. The phrase "producer to consumer" is commonly used by market analysts.
    D. The lawyer shouted, "Is not this evidence illegal?"

6.____

Questions 7-9.

DIRECTIONS: In answering Questions 7 through 9, mark the letter A if faulty because of incorrect grammar, mark the letter B if faulty because of incorrect punctuation, mark the letter C if correct.

7.   Mr. Brown our accountant, will audit the accounts next week.   7._____

8.   Give the assignment to whomever is able to do it most efficiently.   8._____

9.   The supervisor expected either your or I to file these reports.   9._____

Questions 10-14.

DIRECTIONS: In each of the following groups of four sentences, one sentence contains an error in sentence structure, grammar, usage, diction, or punctuation. Indicate the INCORRECT sentence.

10.   A.   The agent asked, "Did you say, 'Never again?"   10._____
       B.   Kindly let me know whether you can visit us on the 17th.
       C.   "I cannot accept that!" he exploded. "Please show me something else."
       D.   Ed, will you please lend me your grass shears for an hour or so.

11.   A.   Recalcitrant though he may have been, Alexander was wilfully destructive.   11._____
       B.   Everybody should look out for himself.
       C.   John is one of those students who usually spends most of his time in the princi-
             pal's office.
       D.   She seems to feel that what is theirs is hers.

12.   A.   Be he ever so much in the wrong, I'll support the man while deploring his actions.   12._____
       B.   The schools' lack of interest in consumer education is shortsighted.
       C.   I think that Fitzgerald's finest stanza is one which includes the reference to
             youth's "sweet-scented manuscript."
       D.   I never would agree to Anderson having full control of the company's policies.

13.   A.   We had to walk about five miles before finding a gas station.   13._____
       B.   The willful sending of a false alarm has, and may, result in homicide.
       C.   Please bring that book to me at once!
       D.   Neither my sister nor I am interested in bowling.

14.   A.   He is one of the very few football players who doesn't wear a helmet with a face   14._____
             guard.
       B.   But three volunteers appeared at the recruiting office.
       C.   Such consideration as you can give us will be appreciated.
       D.   When I left them, the group were disagreeing about the proposed legislation.

Question 15.

DIRECTIONS: Question 15 contains two sentences concerning criminal law. The sentences could contain errors in English grammar or usage. A sentence does not contain an error simply because it could be written in a different manner. In answering this question, choose answer
    A. if only sentence I is correct
    B. if only sentence II is correct
    C. if both sentences are correct
    D. if neither sentence is correct

15.   I.   The use of fire or explosives to destroy tangible property is proscribed by the criminal mischief provisions of the Revised Penal Law.   15._____
    II. The defendant's taking of a taxicab for the immediate purpose of affecting his escape did not constitute grand larceny.

KEY (CORRECT ANSWERS)

1.	A		6.	A
2.	B		7.	B
3.	C		8.	A
4.	B		9.	A
5.	D		10.	A

11.	C
12.	D
13.	B
14.	A
15.	A

PREPARING WRITTEN MATERIAL

PARAGRAPH REARRANGEMENT
COMMENTARY

The sentences that follow are in scrambled order. You are to rearrange them in proper order and indicate the letter choice containing the correct answer at the space at the right.

Each group of sentences in this section is actually a paragraph presented in scrambled order. Each sentence in the group has a place in that paragraph; no sentence is to be left out. You are to read each group of sentences and decide upon the best order in which to put the sentences so as to form a well-organized paragraph.

The questions in this section measure the ability to solve a problem when all the facts relevant to its solution are not given.

More specifically, certain positions of responsibility and authority require the employee to discover connection between events sometimes, apparently, unrelated. In order to do this, the employee will find it necessary to correctly infer that unspecified events have probably occurred or are likely to occur. This ability becomes especially important when action must be taken on incomplete information.

Accordingly, these questions require competitors to choose among several suggested alternatives, each of which presents a different sequential arrangement of the events. Competitors must choose the MOST logical of the suggested sequences.

In order to do so, they may be required to draw on general knowledge to infer missing concepts or events that are essential to sequencing the given events. Competitors should be careful to infer only what is essential to the sequence. The plausibility of the wrong alternatives will always require the inclusion of unlikely events or of additional chains of events which are NOT essential to sequencing the given events.

It's very important to remember that you are looking for the best of the four possible choices, and that the best choice of all may not even be one of the answers you're given to choose from.

There is no one right way to solve these problems. Many people have found it helpful to first write out the order of the sentences, as they would have arranged them, on their scrap paper before looking at the possible answers. If their optimum answer is there, this can save them some time. If it isn't, this method can still give insight into solving the problem. Others find it most helpful to just go through each of the possible choices, contrasting each as they go along. You should use whatever method feels comfortable and works for you.

While most of these types of questions are not that difficult, we've added a higher percentage of the difficult type, just to give you more practice. Usually there are only one or two questions on this section that contain such subtle distinctions that you're unable to answer confidently. And you then may find yourself stuck deciding between two possible choices, neither of which you're sure about.

PREPARING WRITTEN MATERIAL

EXAMINATION SECTION

TEST 1

DIRECTIONS: The following groups of sentences need to be arranged in an order that makes sense. Select the letter preceding the sequence that represents the best sentence order. *PRINT THE LETTER OF THE CORRECT ANSWER IN THE SPACE AT THE RIGHT.*

1. I. The ostrich egg shell's legendary toughness makes it an excellent substitute for certain types of dishes or dinnerware, and in parts of Africa ostrich shells are cut and decorated for use as containers for water.
   II. Since prehistoric times, people have used the enormous egg of the ostrich as a part of their diet, a practice which has required much patience and hard work—to hard boil an ostrich egg takes about four hours.
   III. Opening the egg's shell, which is rock hard and nearly an inch thick, requires heavy tools, such as a saw or chisel; from inside, a baby ostrich must use a hornlike projection on its beak as a miniature pick-axe to escape from the egg.
   IV. The offspring of all higher-order animals originate from single egg cells that are carried by mothers, and most of these eggs are relatively small, often microscopic.
   V. The egg of the African ostrich, however, weighs a massive thirty pounds, making it the largest single cell on earth, and a common object of human curiosity and wonder.
   The BEST order is:
   A. V, IV, I, II, III   B. I, IV, V, III, II   C. IV, II, III, V, I   D. IV, V, II, III, I

   1.____

2. I. Typically only a few feet high on the open sea, individual tsunami have been known to circle the entire globe two or three times if their progress is not interrupted, but are not usually dangerous until they approach the shallow water that surrounds land masses.
   II. Some of the most terrifying and damaging hazards caused by earthquakes are tsunami, which were once called "tidal waves"—a poorly chosen name, since these waves have nothing to do with tides.
   III. Then a wave, slowed by the sudden drag on the lower part of its moving water column, will pile upon itself, sometimes reaching a height of over 100 feet.
   IV. Tsunami (Japanese for "great harbor wave") are seismic waves that are caused by earthquakes near oceanic trenches, and once triggered, can travel up to 600 miles an hour on the open ocean.
   V. A land-shoaling tsunami is capable of extraordinary destruction; some tsunami have deposited large boats miles inland, washed out two-foot-thick seawalls, and scattered locomotive trains over long distances.
   A. IV, I, III, II, V   B. I, III, IV, II, V   C. V, I, III, II, IV   D. II, IV, I, III, V

   2.____

3. I.   Soon, by the 1940s, jazz was the most popular type of music among American intellectuals and college students.
    II. In the early days of jazz, it was considered "lowdown" music, or music that was played only in rough, disreputable bars and taverns.
    III. However, jazz didn't take too long to develop from early ragtime melodies into more complex, sophisticated forms, such as Charlie Parker's "bebop" style of jazz.
    IV. After charismatic band leaders such as Duke Ellington and Count Basie brought jazz to a larger audience, and jazz continued to evolve into more complicated forms, white audiences began to accept and even to enjoy the new American art form.
    V.   Many white Americans, who then dictated the tastes of society, were wary of music that was played almost exclusively in black clubs in the poorer sections of cities and towns.

    The BEST order is:
    A. V, IV, III, II, I   B. II, V, III, IV, I   C. IV, V, III, I, II   D. I, II, IV, III, V

3.____

4. I.   Then, hanging in a windless place, the magnetized end of the needle would always point to the south.
    II. The needle could then be balanced on the rim of a cup, or the edge of a fingernail, but this balancing act was hard to maintain, and the needle often fell off.
    III. Other needles would point to the north, and it was important for any traveler finding his way with a compass to remember which kind of magnetized needle he was carrying.
    IV. To make some of the earliest compasses in recorded history, ancient Chinese "magicians" would rub a needle with a piece of magnetized iron called a lodestone.
    V.   A more effective method of keeping the needle free to swing with its magnetic pull was to attach a strand of silk to the center of the needle with a tiny piece of wax.

    The BEST order is:
    A. IV, II, V, I, III   B. IV, III, V, II, I   C. IV, V, II, I, III   D. IV, I, III, V, II

4.____

5. I   The now-famous first mate of the *H.M.S. Bounty*, Fletcher Christian, founded one of the world's most peculiar civilizations in 1790.
    II. The men knew they had just committed a crime for which they could be hanged, so they set sail for Pitcairn, a remote, abandoned island in the far eastern region of the Polynesian archipelago, accompanied by twelve Polynesian women and six men.
    III. In a mutiny that has become legendary, Christian and the others forced Captain Bligh into a lifeboat and set him adrift off the coast of Tonga in April of 1789.
    IV. In early 1790, the *Bounty* landed at Pitcairn Island, where the men lived out the rest of their lives and founded an isolated community which to this day includes direct descendants of Christian and the other Crewmen.

5.____

V. The *Bounty*, commanded by Captain William Bligh, was in the middle of a global voyage, and Christian and his shipmates had come to the conclusion that Bligh was a reckless madman who would lead them to their deaths unless they took the ship from him.

The BEST order is:

  A. IV, V, III, II, I   B. I, III, V, II, IV   C. I, V, III, II, IV   D. II, I, V, IV, II

6.   I.   But once the vines had been led to make orchids, the flowers had to be carefully hand-pollinated, because unpollinated orchids usually lasted less than a day, wilting and dropping off the vine before it had even become dark.

      II. The Totonac farmers discovered that looping a vine back around once it reached a five-foot height on its host tree would cause the vine to flower.

      III. Though they knew how to process the fruit pods and extract vanilla's flavoring agent, the Totonacs also knew that a wild vanilla vine did not produce abundant flowers or fruit.

      IV. Wild vines climbed along the trunks and canopies of trees, and this constant upward growth diverted most of the vine's energy to making leaves instead of the orchid flowers that once pollinated, would produce the flavorful pods.

      V. Hundreds of years before vanilla became a prized food flavoring in Europe and the Western World, the Totonac Indians of the Mexican Gulf Coast were skilled cultivators of the vanilla vine, whose fruit they literally worshipped as a goddess.

The BEST order is:

  A. II, III, IV, I, V   B. II, IV, III, I, V   C. V, III, IV, II, I   D. III, IV, I, II, V

6.____

7.   I.   Once airborne, the spider is at the mercy of the air currents—usually the spider takes a brief journey, traveling close to the ground, but some have been found in air samples collected as high as 10,000 feet, or been reported landing on ships far out at sea.

      II. Once a young spider has hatched, it must leave the environment into which it was born as quickly as possible, in order to avoid competing with its hundreds of brothers and sisters for food.

      III. The silk rises into warm air currents, and as soon as the pull feels adequate the spider lets go and drifts up into the air, suspended from the silk strand in the same way that a person might parasail.

      IV. To help young spiders do this, many species have adapted a practice known as "aerial dispersal," or, in common speech, "ballooning."

      V. A spider that wants to leave its surroundings quickly will climb to the top of a grass system or twig, face into the wind, and aim its back end into the air, releasing a long stream of silk from the glands near the tip of its abdomen.

The BEST order is:

  A. V, IV, II, III, I   B. V, II, IV, I, III   C. II, V, IV, III, I   D. II, IV, V, III, I

7.____

8. I. For about a year, Tycho worked at a castle in Prague with a scientist named Johannes Kepler, but their association was cut short by another argument that drove Kepler out of the castle, to later develop, on his own, the theory of planetary orbits.

    II. Tycho found life without a nose embarrassing, so he made a new nose for himself out of silver, which reportedly remained glued to his face for the rest of his life.

    III. Tycho Brahe, the 17th-century Danish astronomer, is today more famous for his odd and arrogant personality than for any contribution he has made to our knowledge of the stars and planets.

    IV. Early in his career, as a student at Rostock University, Tycho got into an argument with another student about who was the better mathematician, and the two became so angry that the argument turned into a sword fight, during which Tycho's nose was sliced off.

    V. Later in his life, Tycho's arrogance may have kept him from playing a part in one of the greatest astronomical discoveries in history: the elliptical orbits of the solar system's planets.

    The BEST order is:
      A. I, IV, II, III, V   B. IV, II, III, V, I   C. IV, II, I, III, V   D. III, IV, II, V, I

8.____

9. I. The processionaries are so used to this routine that if a person picks up the end of a silk line and brings it back to the origin—creating a closed circle—the caterpillars may travel around and around for days, sometimes starving or freezing, without changing course.

    II. Rather than relying on sight or sound, the other caterpillars, who are lined up end-to-end behind the leader, travel to and from their nests by walking on this silk line, and each will reinforce it by laying down its own marking line as it passes over.

    III. In order to insure the safety of individuals, the processionary caterpillar nests in a tree with dozens of other caterpillars, and at night, when it is safest, they all leave together in search of food.

    IV. The processionary caterpillar of the European continent is a perfect illustration of how much some inspect species rely on instinct in their daily routines.

    V. As they leave their nests, the processionaries form a single-file line behind a leader who spins and lays out a silk line to mark the chosen path.

    The BEST order is:
      A. IV, III, V, II, I   B. III, V, IV, II, I   C. III, V, II, I, IV   D. IV, V, III, I, II

9.____

10. I. Often, the child is also given a handcrafted walker or push cart, to provide support for its first upright explorations.

    II. In traditional Indian families, a child's first steps are celebrated as a ceremonial event, rooted in ancient myth.

    III. These carts are often intricately designed to resemble the chariot of Krishna, an important figure in Indian mythology.

    IV. The sound of these anklet bells is intended to mimic the footsteps of the legendary child Rama, who is celebrated in devotional songs throughout India.

10.____

V. When the child's parents see that the child is ready to begin walking, they will fit it with specially designed ankle bracelets, adorned with gently ringing bells.

The BEST order is:

A. II, III, IV, I, V   B. II, V, III, I, IV   C. V, IV, I, III, II   D. V, III, II, I, IV

11.

I. The settlers planted Osage oranges all across Middle America, and today long lines and rectangles of Osage orange trees can still be seen on the prairies, running along the former boundaries of farms that no longer exist.

II. After trying sod walls and water-filled ditches with no success, American farmers began to look for a plant that was adaptable to prairie weather, and that could be trimmed into a hedge that was "pig-tight, horse-high, and bull-strong."

III. The tree, so named because it bore a large (but inedible) fruit the size of an orange, was among the sturdiest and hardiest of American trees, and was prized among Native Americans for the strength and flexibility of bows which were made from its wood.

IV. The first people to practice agriculture on the American flatlands were faced with an important problem: what would they use to fence their land in a place that was almost entirely without trees or rocks?

V. Finally, an Illinois farmer brought the settlers a tree that was native to the land between the Red and Arkansas rivers, a tree called the Osage orange.

The BEST order is:

A. II, I, V, III, IV   B. I, II, III, IV, V   C. IV, II, V, III, I   D. IV, II, I, III, V

11.____

12.

I. After about ten minutes of such spirited and complicated activity, the head dancer is free to make up his or her own movements while maintaining the interest of the New Year's crowd.

II. The dancer will then perform a series of leg kicks, while at the same time operating the lion's mouth with his own hand and moving the ears and eyes by means of a string which is attached to the dancer's own mouth.

III. The most difficult role of this dance belongs to the one who controls the lion's head; this person must lead all the other "parts" of the lion through the choreographed segments of the dance.

IV. The head dancer begins with a complex series of steps. alternately stepping forward with the head raised, and then retreating a few steps while lowering the head, a movement that is intended to create the impression that the lion is keeping a watchful eye for anything evil.

V. When performing a traditional Chinese New Year's lion dance, several performers must fit themselves inside a large lion costume and work together to enact different parts of the dance.

The BEST order is:

A. V, III, IV, II, I   B. III, IV, II, V, I   C. III, I, V, IV, II   D. IV, II, III, V, I

12.____

13. I.   For many years the shell of the chambered nautilus was treasured in Europe for its beauty and intricacy, but collectors were unaware that they were in possession of the structure that marked a "missing link" in the evolution of marine mollusks.

    II. The nautilus, however, evolved a series of enclosed chambers in its shell, and invented a new use for the structure: the shell began to serve as a buoyancy device.

    III. Equipped with this new flotation device, the nautilus did not need the single, muscular foot of its predecessors, but instead developed flaps, tentacles, and a gentle form of jet propulsion that transformed it into the first mollusk able to take command of its own density and explore a three-dimensional world.

    IV. By pumping and adjusting air pressure into the chambers, the nautilus could spend the day resting on the bottom, and then rise toward the surface at night in search of food.

    V.   The nautilus shell looks like a large snail shell, similar to those of its ancestors, who used their shells as protective coverings while they were anchored to the sea floor.

    The BEST order is:
    A. V, II, IV, I, III   B. V, I, II, III, IV   C. I, II, V, III, IV   D. I, V, II, IV, III

    13.____

14. I.   While France and England battled for control of the region, the Acadiens prospered on the fertile farmland, which was finally secured by England in 1713.

    II. Early in the 17th century, settlers from Western France founded a colony called Acadie in what is now the Canadian province of Nova Scotia.

    III. At this time, English officials feared the presence of spies among the Acadiens who might be loyal to their French homeland, and the Acadiens were deported to spots along the Atlantic and Caribbean shores of America.

    IV. The French settlers remained on this land, under English rule, for around forty years, until the beginning of the French and Indian War, another conflict between France and England.

    V.   As the Acadien refugees drifted toward a final home in Southern Louisiana, neighbors shortened their name to "Cadien," and finally "Cajun," the name which the descendants of early Acadiens still call themselves.

    The BEST order is:
    A. I, IV, II, III, V   B. II, I, III, V, IV   C. II, I, IV, III, V   D. V, II, III, IV, I

    14.____

15. I.   Traditiona households in the Eastern and Western regions of Africa serve to meals a daay—one at around noon, and the other in the evening.

    II. The starch is then used in the way that Americans might use a spoon, to scoop up a portion of the main dish on the person's plate.

    III. The reason for the starch's inclusion in every meal has to do with taste as well as nutrition; African food can be very spicy, and the starch is known to cool the burning effect of the main dish.

    IV. When serving these meals, the main dish is usually served on individual plates, and the starch is served on a communal plate, from which diners break off a piece of bread or scoop rice or fufu in their fingers.

    15.____

V. The typical meals usually consist of a thick stew or soup as the main course, and an accompanying starch—either bread, rice, or *fufu*, a starchy grain paste similar in consistency to mashed potatoes.

The BEST order is:

A. V, II, III, IV, I   B. V, I, IV, III, II   C. I, IV, V, III, II   D. I, V, IV, II, III

16.   I. In the early days of the American Midwest, Indiana settlers sometimes came together to hold an event called an apple peeling, where neighboring settlers gathered at the homestead of a host family to help prepare the hosts' apple crop for cooking, canning, and making apple butter.

      II. At the beginning of the event, each peeler sat down in front of a ten- or twenty-gallon stone jar and was given a crock of apples and a paring knife.

     III. Once a peeler had finished with a crock, another was placed next to him; if the peeler was an unmarried man, he kept a strict count of the number of apples he had peeled, because the winner was allowed to kiss the girl of his choice.

     IV. The peeling usually ended by 9:30 in the evening, when the neighbors gathered in the host family's parlor for a dance social.

     V. The apples were peeled, cored, and quartered, and then placed into the jar.

The BEST order is:

A. I, V, III, IV, II   B. II, V, III, IV, I   C. I, II, V, III, IV   D. II, I, V, IV, III

16.____

17.   I. If your pet turtle is a land turtle and is native to temperate climates, it will stop eating some time in October, which should be your cue to prepare the turtle for hibernation.

      II. The box should then be covered with a wire screen, which will protect the turtle from any rodents or predators that might want to take advantage of a motionless and helpless animal.

     III. When your turtle hasn't eaten for a while and appears ready to hibernate, it should be moved to its winter quarters, most likely a cellar or garage, where the temperature should range between 40° and 45°F.

     IV. Instead of feeding the turtle, you should bathe it every day in warm water, to encourage the turtle to empty its intestines in preparation for its long winter sleep.

     V. Here the turtle should be placed in a well-ventilated box whose bottom is covered with a moisture-absorbing layer of clay beads, and then filled three-fourths full with almost dry peat moss or wood chips, into which the turtle will burrow and sleep for several months.

The BEST order is:

A. I, IV, III, V, II   B. III, IV, II, V, I   C. III, II, IV, I, V   D. IV, V, II, III, I

17.____

18.   I. Once he has reached the nest, the hunter uses two sturdy bamboo poles like huge chopsticks to pull the next away from the mountainside, into a large basket that will be lowered to people waiting below.

      II. The world's largest honeybees colonize the Nealese mountainsides, building honeycombs as large as a person on sheer rock faces that are often hundreds of feet high.

18.____

III. In the remote mountain country of Nepal, a small band of "honey hunters" carry out a tradition so ancient that 10,000 year-old drawings of the practice have been found in the caves of Nepal.

IV. To harvest the honey and beeswax from these combs, a honey hunter climbs above the nests, lowers a long bamboo-fiber ladder over the cliff, and then climbs down.

V. Throughout this dangerous practice, the hunter is stung repeatedly, and only the veterans, with skin that has been toughened over the years, are able to return from a hunt without the painful swelling caused by stings.

The BEST order is:

  A. II, IV, III, V, I   B. II, IV, I, V, III   C. V, III, II, IV, I   D. III, II, IV, I, V

19. I. After the Romans left Britain, there were relentless attacks on the islands from the barbarian tribes of northern Germany—the Angles, Saxons, and Jutes.

II. As the empire weakened, Roman soldiers withdrew from Britain, leaving behind a country that continued to practice the Christian religion that had been introduced by the Romans.

III. Early Latin writings tell of a Christian warrior named Arturius (Arthur, in English) who led the British citizens to defeat these barbarian invades, and brought an extended period of peace to the lands of Britain.

IV. Long ago, the British Isles were part of the far-flung Roman Empire that extended across most of Europe and into Africa and Asia.

V. The romantic legend of King Arthur and his knights of the Round Table, one of the most popular and widespread stories of all time, appears to have some foundation in history.

The BEST order is:

  A. V, IV, III, II, I   B. V, IV, II, I, III   C. IV, V, II, III, I   D. IV, III, II, I, V

19._____

20. I. The cylinder was allowed to cool until it could stand on its own, and then it was cut from the tube and split down the side with a single straight cut.

II. Nineteenth-century glassmakers, who had not yet discovered the glazier's modern techniques for making panes of glass, had to create a method for converting their blown gas into flat sheets.

III. The bubble was then pierced at the end to make a hole that opened up while the glassmaker gently spun it, creating a cylinder of glass.

IV. Turned on its side and laid on a conveyor belt, the cylinder was strengthened, or tempered, by being heated again and cooled very slowly, eventually flattening out into a single rectangular of glass.

V. To do this, the glassmaker dipped the end of a long tube into melted glass and blew into the other end of the tube, creating an expanding bubble of glass.

The BEST order is:

  A. II, V, III, IV, I   B. II, IV, V, III, I   C. III, V, II, IV, I   D. III, I, IV, V, II

20._____

21. I.   The splints are almost always hidden, but horses are occasionally born whose splinted toes project from the leg on either side, just above the hoof.
     II. The second and fourth toes remained, but shrank to thin splints of bone that fused invisibly to the horse's leg bone.
     III. Horses are unique among mammals, having evolved feet that each end in what is essentially a single toe, capped by a large, sturdy hoof.
     IV. Julius Caesar, an emperor of ancient Rome, was said to have owned one of these three-toed horses, and considered it so special that he would not permit anyone else to ride it.
     V.   Though the horse's earlier ancestors possessed the traditional mammalian set of five toes on each foot, the horse has retained only its third toe; its first and fifth toes disappeared completely as the horse evolved.

     The BEST order is:

     A. III, V, II, I, IV   B. V, III, II, IV, I   C. III, II, V, I, IV   D. V, II, III, I, IV

21.____

22. I.   The new building materials—some of which are twenty feet long, and weigh nearly six tons—were transported to Pohnpei on rafts, and were brought into their present position by using hibiscus fiber ropes and leverage to move the stone columns upward along the inclined trunks of coconut palm trees.
     II. The ancestors built great fires to heat the stone, and then poured cool seawater on the columns, which caused the stone to contract and split along natural fracture lines.
     III. The now-abandoned enclave of Nan Madol, a group of 92 man-made islands off the shore of the Micronesian island of Pohnpei, is estimated to have been built around the year 500 A.D.
     IV. The islanders say their ancestors quarried stone columns from a nearby island, where large basalt columns were formed by the cooling of molten lava.
     V.   The structures of Nan Madol are remarkable for the sheer size of some of the stone "longs" or columns that were used to create the walls of the offshore community, and today anthropologists can only rely on the information of existing local people for clues about how Nan Madol was built.

     The BEST order is:

     A. V, IV, III, II, I   B. V, III, I, IV, II   C. III, V, IV, II, I   D. III, I, IV, II, V

22.____

23. I.   One of the most easily manipulated substances on earth, glass can be made into ceramic tiles that are composed of over 90% air.
     II. NASA's space shuttles are the first spacecraft ever designed to leave and re-enter the earth's atmosphere while remaining intact.
     III. These ceramic tiles are such effective insulators that when a tile emerges from the oven in which it was fired, it can be held safely in a person's hand by the edges while its interior still glows at a temperature well over 2000°F.
     IV. Eventually, the engineers were led to a material that is as old as our most ancient civilization.
     V.   Because the temperature during atmospheric re-entry is so incredibly hot, it took NASA's engineers some time to find a substance capable of protecting the shuttles.

22.____

The BEST order is:
  A. V, II, I, II, IV   B. II, V, IV, I, III   C. II, III, I, IV, V   D. V, V, III, I, II

24. I. The secret to teaching any parakeet to talk is patience, and the understanding that when a bird talks," it is simply imitating what it hears, rather than putting ideas into words.
    II. You should stay just out of sight of the bird and repeat the phrase you want it to learn, for at least fifteen minutes every morning and evening.
    III. It is important to leave the bird without any words of encouragement or farewell; otherwise it might combine stray remarks or phrases, such as "Good night," with the phrase you are trying to teach it.
    IV. For this reason, to train your bird to imitate your words you should keep it free of any distractions, especially other noises, while you are giving it "lesson."
    V. After your repetition, you should quietly leave the bird alone for a while, to think over what it has just heard.

The BEST order is:
  A. I, IV, II, V, III   B. I, II, IV, III, V   C. III, II, I, V, IV   D. III, I, V, IV, II

25. I. As a school approaches, fishermen from neighboring communities join their fishing boats together as a fleet, and string their gill nets together to make a huge fence that is held up by cork floats.
    II. At a signal from the party leaders, or *nakura*, the family members pound the sides of the boats or beat the water with long poles, creating a sudden and deafening noise.
    III. The fishermen work together to drag the trap into a half-circle that may reach 300 yards in diameter, and then the families move their boats to form the other half of the circle around the school of fish.
    IV. The school of fish flee from the commotion into the awaiting trap, where a final wall of net is thrown over the open end of the half-circle, securing the day's haul.
    V. Indonesian people from the area around the Sulu islands live on the sea, in floating villages made of lashed-together or stilted homes, and make much of their living by fishing their home waters for migrating schools of snapper, scad, and other fish.

The BEST order is:
  A. I, V, III, IV, II   B. I, II, IV, III, V   C. V, I, II, III, IV   D. V, I, III, II, IV

KEY (CORRECT ANSWERS)

1.	D		11.	C
2.	D		12.	A
3.	B		13.	D
4.	A		14.	C
5.	C		15.	D
6.	C		16.	C
7.	D		17.	A
8.	D		18.	D
9.	A		19.	B
10.	B		20.	A

21.	A
22.	C
23.	B
24.	A
25.	D

EXAMINATION SECTION
TEST 1

DIRECTIONS: In each of the following questions, only one of the four sentences conforms to standards of correct usage. The other three contain errors in grammar, diction, or punctuation. Select the choice in each question which BEST conforms to standards of correct usage. Consider a choice correct if it contains none of the errors mentioned above, even though there may be other ways of expressing the same thought. *PRINT THE LETTER OF THE CORRECT ANSWER IN THE SPACE AT THE RIGHT.*

1.   A. Because he was ill was no excuse for his behavior   1._____
     B. In insist that he see a lawyer before he goes to trial.
     C. He said "that he had not intended to go."
     D. He wasn't out of the office only three days.

2.   A. He came to the station and pays a porter to carry his bags into the train.   2._____
     B. I should have liked to live in medieval times.
     C. My father was born in Linville. A little country town where everybody knows everyone else.
     D. The car, which is parked across the street, is disabled.

3.   A. He asked the desk clerk for a clean, quiet, room.   3._____
     B. I expected James to be lonesome and that he would want to go home.
     C. I have stopped worrying because I have heard nothing further on the subject.
     D. If the board of directors controls the company, they may take actions which are disapproved by the stockholders.

4.   A. Each of the players knew their place.   4._____
     B. He whom you saw on the stage is the son of an actor.
     C. Susan is the smartest of the twin sisters.
     D. Who ever thought of him winning both prizes?

5.   A. An outstanding trait of early man was their reliance on omens.   5._____
     B. Because I had never been there before.
     C. Neither Mr. Jones nor Mr. Smith has completed his work.
     D. While eating my dinner, a dog came to the window.

6.   A. A copy of the lease, in addition to the Rules and Regulations, are to be given to each tenant.   6._____
     B. The Rules and Regulations and a copy of the lease is being given to each tenant.
     C. A copy of the lease, in addition to the Rules and Regulations, is to be given to each tenant.
     D. A copy of the lease, in addition to the Rules and Regulations, are being given to each tenant.

7. A. Although we understood that for him music was a passion, we were disturbed by the fact that he was addicted to sing along with the soloists.
    B. Do you believe that Steven is liable to win a scholarship?
    C. Give the picture to whomever is a connoisseur of art.
    D. Whom do you believe to be the most efficient worker in the office?

7._____

8. A. Each adult who is sure they know all the answers will some day realize their mistake.
    B. Even the most hardhearted villain would have to feel bad about so horrible a tragedy.
    C. Neither being licensed teachers, both aspirants had to pass rigorous tests before being appointed.
    D. The principal reason why he wanted to be designated was because he had never before been to a convention.

8.____

9. A. Being that the weather was so inclement, the party has been postponed for at least a month.
    B. He is in New York City only three weeks and he has already seen all the thrilling sights in Manhattan and in the other four boroughs.
    C. If you will look it up in the official directory, which can be consulted in the library during specified hours, you will discover that the chairman and director are Mr. T. Henry Long.
    D. Working hard at college during the day and at the post office during the night, he appeared to his family to be indefatigable.

9.____

10. A. I would have been happy to oblige you if you only asked me to do it.
    B. The cold weather, as well as the unceasing wind and rain, have made us decide to spend the winter in Florida.
    C. The politician would have been more successful in winning office if he would have been less dogmatic.
    D. These trousers are expensive; however, they will wear well.

10.____

11. A. All except him wore formal attire at the reception for the ambassador.
    B. If that chair were to be blown off of the balcony, it might injure someone below.
    C. Not a passenger, who was in the crash, survived the impact.
    D. To borrow money off friends is the best way to lose them.

11.____

12. A. Approaching Manhattan on the ferry boat from Staten Island, an unforgettable sight of the skyscrapers is seen.
    B. Did you see the exhibit of modernistic paintings as yet?
    C. Gesticulating wildly and ranting in stentorian tones, the speaker was the sinecure of all eyes.
    D. The airplane with crew and passengers was lost somewhere in the Pacific Ocean.

12.____

13. A. If one has consistently had that kind of training, it is certainly too late to change your entire method of swimming long distances.
    B. The captain would have been more impressed if you would have been more conscientious in evacuation drills.
    C. The passengers on the stricken ship were all ready to abandon it at the signal.
    D. The villainous shark lashed at the lifeboat with it's tail, trying to upset the rocking boat in order to partake of it's contents.

13.____

14. A. As one whose been certified as a professional engineer, I believe that the decision to build a bridge over that harbor is unsound.
    B. Between you and me, this project ought to be completed long before winter arrives.
    C. He fervently hoped that the men would be back at camp and to find them busy at their usual chores.
    D. Much to his surprise, he discovered that the climate of Korea was like his home town.

14.____

15. A. An industrious executive is aided, not impeded, by having a hobby which gives him a fresh point of view on life and its problems.
    B. Frequent absence during the calendar year will surely mitigate against the chances of promotion.
    C. He was unable to go to the committee meeting because he was very ill.
    D. Mr. Brown expressed his disapproval so emphatically that his associates were embarassed

15.____

16. A. At our next session, the office manager will have told you something about his duties and responsibilities.
    B. In general, the book is absorbing and original and have no hesitation about recommending it.
    C. The procedures followed by private industry in dealing with lateness and absence are different from ours.
    D We shall treat confidentially any information about Mr. Doe, to whom we understand you have sent reports to for many years.

16.____

17. A. I talked to one official, whom I knew was fully impartial.
    B. Everyone signed the petition but him.
    C. He proved not only to be a good student but also a good athlete.
    D. All are incorrect.

17.____

18. A. Every year a large amount of tenants are admitted to housing projects.
    B. Henry Ford owned around a billion dollars in industrial equipment.
    C. He was aggravated by the child's poor behavior.
    D. All are incorrect.

18.____

89

19. A. Before he was committed to the asylum he suffered from the illusion that he was Napoleon.
    B. Besides stocks, there were also bonds in the safe.
    C. We bet the other team easily.
    D. All are incorrect.

19.____

20. A. Bring this report to your supervisory.
    B. He set the chair down near the table.
    C. The capitol of New York is Albany.
    D. All are incorrect.

20.____

21. A. He was chosen to arbitrate the dispute because everyone knew he would be disinterested.
    B. It is advisable to obtain the best council before making an important decision.
    C. Less college students are interested in teaching than ever before.
    D. All are incorrect.

21.____

22. A. She, hearing a signal, the source lamp flashed.
    B. While hearing a signal, the source lamp flashed.
    C. In hearing a signal, the source lamp flashed.
    D. As she heard a signal, the source lamp flashed.

22.____

23. A. Every one of the time records have been initialed in the designated spaces.
    B. All of the time records has been initialed in the designated spaces.
    C. Each one of the time records was initialed in the designated spaces.
    D. The time records all been initialed in the designated spaces.

23.____

24. A. If there is no one else to answer the phone, you will have to answer it.
    B. You will have to answer it yourself if no one else answers the phone.
    C. If no one else is not around to pick up the phone, you will have to do it.
    D. You will have to answer the phone when nobodys here to do it.

24.____

25. A. Dr. Barnes not in his office. What could I do for you?
    B. Dr. Barnes is not in his office. Is there something I can do for you?
    C. Since Dr. Barnes is not in his office, might there be something I may do for you?
    D. Is there any ways I can assist you since Dr. Barnes is not in his office?

25.____

26. A. She do not understand how the new console works.
    B. The way the new console works, she doesn't understand.
    C. She doesn't understand how the new console works.
    D. The new console works, so that she doesn't understand.

26.____

27. A. Certain changes in my family income must be reported as they occur.
    B. When certain changes in family income occur, it must be reported.
    C. Certain family income change must be reported as they occur.
    D. Certain changes in family income must be reported as they have been occurring.

27.____

28. A. Each tenant has to complete the application themselves.
    B. Each of the tenants have to complete the application by himself.
    C. Each of the tenants has to complete the application himself.
    D. Each of the tenants has to complete the application by themselves.

28.____

29. A. Yours is the only building that the construction will effect.
    B. Your's is the only building affected by the construction.
    C. The construction will only effect your building.
    D. Yours is the only building that will be affected by the construction.

29.____

30. A. There is four tests left.
    B. The number of tests left are four.
    C. There are four tests left.
    D. Four of the tests remains.

30.____

31. A. Each of the applicants takes a test.
    B. Each of the applicant take a test.
    C. Each of the applicants take tests.
    D. Each of the applicants have taken tests.

31.____

32. A. The applicant, not the examiners, are ready.
    B. The applicants, not the examiners, is ready.
    C. The applicants, not the examiner, are ready.
    D. The applicant, not the examiner, are ready

32.____

33. A. You will not progress except you practice.
    B. You will not progress without you practicing.
    C. You will not progress unless you practice.
    D. You will not progress provided you do not practice.

33.____

34. A. Neither the director or the employees will be at the office tomorrow.
    B. Neither the director nor the employees will be at the office tomorrow.
    C. Neither the director, or the secretary nor the other employees will be at the office tomorrow.
    D. Neither the director, the secretary or the other employees will be at the office tomorrow.

34.____

35. A. In my absence, he and her will have to finish the assignment.
    B. In my absence he and she will have to finish the assignment.
    C. In my absence she and him, they will have to finish the assignment.
    D. In my absence he and her both will have to finish the assignment.

35.____

KEY (CORRECT ANSWERS)

1.	B	11.	A	21.	A	31.	A
2.	B	12.	D	22.	D	32.	C
3.	C	13.	C	23.	C	33.	C
4.	B	14.	B	24.	A	34.	B
5.	C	15.	A	25.	B	35.	B
6.	C	16.	C	26.	C		
7.	D	17.	B	27.	A		
8.	B	18.	D	28.	C		
9.	D	19.	B	29.	D		
10.	D	20.	B	30.	C		

TEST 2

DIRECTIONS: Each question or incomplete statement is followed by several suggested answers or completions. Select the one that BEST answers the question or completes the statement. *PRINT THE LETTER OF THE CORRECT ANSWER IN THE SPACE AT THE RIGHT.*

Questions 1-4.

DIRECTIONS: Questions 1 through 4 consist of three sentences each. For each question, select the sentence which contains NO error in grammar or usage.

1.   A.   Be sure that everybody brings his notes to the conference.   1.____
     B.   He looked like he meant to hit the boy.
     C.   Mr. Jones is one of the clients who was chosen to represent the district.
     D.   All are incorrect.

2.   A.   He is taller than I.   2.____
     B.   I'll have nothing to do with these kind of people.
     C.   The reason why he will not buy the house is because it is too expensive.
     D.   All are incorrect.

3.   A.   Aren't I eligible for this apartment.   3.____
     B.   Have you seen him anywheres?
     C.   He should of come earlier.
     D.   All are incorrect.

4.   A.   He graduated college in 1982.   4.____
     B.   He hadn't but one more line to write.
     C.   Who do you think is the author of this report?
     D.   All are incorrect.

Questions 5-35.

DIRECTIONS: In each of the following questions, only one of the four sentences conforms to standards of correct usage. The other three contain errors in grammar, diction, or punctuation. Select the choice in each question which BEST conforms to standards of correct usage. Consider a choice correct if it contains none of the errors mentioned above, even though there may be other ways of expressing the same thought.

5.   A.   It is obvious that no one wants to be a kill-joy if they can help it.   5.____
     B.   It is not always possible, and perhaps it never is possible, to judge a person's character by just looking at him.
     C.   When Yogi Berra of the New York Yankees hit an immortal grandslam home run, everybody in the huge stadium including Pittsburgh fans, rose to his feet.
     D.   Every one of us students must pay tuition today.

93

6.   A. The physician told the young mother that if the baby is not able to digest its milk, it should be boiled.
   B. There is no doubt whatsoever that he felt deeply hurt because John Smith had betrayed the trust.
   C. Having partaken of a most delicious repast prepared by Tessie Breen, the hostess, the horses were driven home immediately thereafter.
   D. The attorney asked my wife and myself several questions.

6.____

7.   A. Despite all denials, there is no doubt in my mind that
   B. At this time everyone must deprecate the demogogic attack made by one of our Senators on one of our most revered statesmen.
   C. In the first game of a crucial two-game series, Ted Williams, got two singles, both of them driving in a run.
   D. Our visitor brought good news to John and I.

7.____

8.   A. If he would have told me, I should have been glad to help him in his dire financial emergency.
   B. Newspaper men have often asserted that diplomats or so-called official spokesmen sometimes employ equivocation in attempts to deceive.
   C. I think someones coming to collect money for the Red Cross.
   D. In a masterly summation, the young attorney expressed his belief that the facts clearly militate against this opinion.

8.____

9.   A. We have seen most all the exhibits.
   B. Without in the least underestimating your advice, in my opinion the situation has grown immeasurably worse in the past few days.
   C. I wrote to the box office treasurer of the hit show that a pair of orchestra seats would be preferable.
   D. As the grim story of Pearl Harbor was broadcast on that fateful December 7, it was the general opinion that war was inevitable.

9.____

10.   A. Without a moment's hesitation, Casey Stengel said that Larry Berra works harder than any player on the team.
   B. There is ample evidence to indicate that many animals can run faster than any human being.
   C. No one saw the accident but I.
   D. Example of courage is the heroic defense put up by the paratroopers against overwhelming odds.

10.____

11.   A. If you prefer these kind, Mrs. Grey, we shall be more than willing to let you have them reasonably.
   B. If you like these here, Mrs. Grey, we shall be more than willing to let you have them reasonably.
   C. If you like these, Mrs. Grey, we shall be more than willing to let you have them.
   D. Who shall we appoint?

11.____

12. A. The number of errors are greater in speech than in writing.
     B. The doctor rather than the nurse was to blame for his being neglected.
     C. Because the demand for these books have been so great, we reduced the price.
     D. John Galsworthy, the English novelist, could not have survived a serious illness; had it not been for loving care.

12.____

13. A. Our activities this year have seldom ever been as interesting as they have been this month.
     B. Our activities this month have been more interesting, or at least as interesting as those of any month this year.
     C. Our activities this month has been more interesting than those of any other month this year.
     D. Neither Jean nor her sister was at home.

13.____

14. A. George B. Shaw's view of common morality, as well as his wit sparkling with a dash of perverse humor here and there, have led critics to term him "The Incurable Rebel."
     B. The President's program was not always received with the wholehearted endorsement of his own party, which is why the party faces difficulty in drawing up a platform for the coming election.
     C. The reason why they wanted to travel was because they had never been away from home.
     D. Facing a barrage of cameras, the visiting celebrity found it extremely difficult to express his opinions clearly.

14.____

15. A. When we calmed down, we all agreed that our anger had been kind of unnecessary and had not helped the situation.
     B. Without him going into all the details, he made us realize the horror of the accident.
     C. Like one girl, for example, who applied for two positions.
     D. Do not think that you have to be so talented as he is in order to play in the school orchestra.

15.____

16. A. He looked very peculiarly to me.
     B. He certainly looked at me peculiar.
     C. Due to the train's being late, we had to wait an hour.
     D. The reason for the poor attendance is that it is raining.

16.____

17. A. About one out of four own an automobile.
     B. The collapse of the old Mitchell Bridge was caused by defective construction in the central pier.
     C. Brooks Atkinson was well acquainted with the best literature, thus helping him to become an able critic.
     D. He has to stand still until the relief man comes up, thus giving him no chance to move about and keep warm.

17.____

18. A. He is sensitive to confusion and withdraws from people whom he feels are too noisy.
     B. Do you know whether the data is statistically correct?
     C. Neither the mayor or the aldermen are to blame.
     D. Of those who were graduated from high school, a goodly percentage went to college.

18.____

19. A. Acting on orders, the offices were searched by a designated committee.
     B. The answer probably is nothing.
     C. I thought it to be all right to excuse them from class.
     D. I think that he is as successful a singer, if not more successful, than Mary.

19.____

20. A. $120,000 is really very little to pay for such a wellbuilt house.
     B. The creatures looked like they had come from outer space.
     C. It was her, he knew!
     D. Nobody but me knows what to do.

20.____

21. A. Mrs. Smith looked good in her new suit.
     B. New York may be compared with Chicago.
     C. I will not go to the meeting except you go with me.
     D. I agree with this editorial.

21.____

22. A. My opinions are different from his.
     B. There will be less students in class now.
     C. Helen was real glad to find her watch.
     D. It had been pushed off of her dresser.

22.____

23. A. Almost everyone, who has been to California, returns with glowing reports.
     B. George Washington, John Adams, and Thomas Jefferson, were our first presidents.
     C. Mr. Walters, whom we met at the bank yesterday, is the man, who gave me my first job.
     D. One should study his lessons as carefully as he can.

23.____

24. A. We had such a good time yesterday.
     B. When the bell rang, the boys and girls went in the schoolhouse.
     C. John had the worst headache when he got up this morning.
     D. Today's assignment is somewhat longer than yesterday's.

24.____

25. A. Neither the mayor nor the city clerk are willing to talk.
     B. Neither the mayor nor the city clerk is willing to talk.
     C. Neither the mayor or the city clerk are willing to talk.
     D Neither the mayor or the city clerk is willing to talk.

25.____

26. A. Being that he is that kind of boy, cooperation cannot be expected.
     B. He interviewed people who he thought had something to say.
     C. Stop whomever enters the building regardless of rank or office held.
     D. Passing through the countryside, the scenery pleased us.

26.____

27. A. The childrens' shoes were in their closet.
    B. The children's shoes were in their closet.
    C. The childs' shoes were in their closet.
    D. The childs' shoes were in his closet.

27.____

28. A. An agreement was reached between the defendant, the plaintiff, the plaintiff's attorney and the insurance company as to the amount of the settlement.
    B. Everybody was asked to give their versions of the accident.
    C. The consensus of opinion was that the evidence was inconclusive.
    D. The witness stated that if he was rich, he wouldn't have had to loan the money.

28.____

29. A. Before beginning the investigation, all the materials related to the case were carefully assembled.
    B. The reason for his inability to keep the appointment is because of his injury in the accident.
    C. This here evidence tends to support the claim of the defendant.
    D. We interviewed all the witnesses who, according to the driver, were still in town.

29.____

30. A. Each claimant was allowed the full amount of their medical expenses.
    B. Either of the three witnesses is available.
    C. Every one of the witnesses was asked to tell his story.
    D. Neither of the witnesses are right.

30.____

31. A. The commissioner, as well as his deputy and various bureau heads, were present.
    B. A new organization of employers and employees have been formed.
    C. One or the other of these men have been selected.
    D. The number of pages in the book is enough to discourage a reader.

31.____

32. A. Between you and me, I think he is the better man.
    B. He was believed to be me.
    C. Is it us that you wish to see?
    D. The winners are him and her.

32.____

33. A. Beside the statement to the police, the witness spoke to no one.
    B. He made no statement other than to the police and I.
    C. He made no statement to any one else, aside from the police.
    D. The witness spoke to no one but me.

33.____

34. A. The claimant has no one to blame but himself.
    B. The boss sent us, he and I, to deliver the packages.
    C. The lights come from mine and not his car.
    D. There was room on the stairs for him and myself.

34.____

35. A. Admission to this clinic is limited to patients' inability to pay for medical
        care.
     B. Patients who can pay little or nothing for medical care are treated in this
        clinic.
     C. The patient's ability to pay for medical care is the determining factor in his
        admission to this clinic.
     D. This clinic is for the patient's that cannot afford to pay or that can pay a little
        for medical care.

35.____

KEY (CORRECT ANSWERS)

1.	A	11.	C	21.	A	31.	D
2.	A	12.	B	22.	A	32.	A
3.	D	13.	D	23.	D	33.	D
4.	C	14.	D	24.	D	34.	A
5.	D	15.	D	25.	B	35.	B
6.	D	16.	D	26.	B		
7.	B	17.	B	27.	B		
8.	B	18.	D	28.	C		
9.	D	19.	B	29.	D		
10.	B	20.	D	30.	C		

EXAMINATION SECTION
TEST 1

DIRECTIONS: Each question or incomplete statement is followed by several suggested answers or completions. Select the one that BEST answers the question or completes the statement. *PRINT THE LETTER OF THE CORRECT ANSWER IN THE SPACE AT THE RIGHT.*

Questions 1-25.

A student has written an article for the high school newspaper, using the skills learned in a stenography and typewriting class in its preparation. In the article which follows, certain words or groups of words are underlined and numbered. The underlined word or group of words may be incorrect because they present an error in grammar, usage, sentence structure, capitalization, diction, or punctuation. For each numbered word or group of words, there is an identically numbered question consisting of four choices based only on the underlined portion. Indicate the BEST choice. Unnecessary changes will be considered incorrect.

TIGERS VIE FOR CITY CHAMPIONSHIP

In their second year of varsity football, the North Side Tigers have gained a shot at the city championship. Last Saturday in the play-offs, the Tigers defeated the Western High
                                        (1)
School Cowboys, thus eliminated that team from contention. Most of the credit for the
                                                                            (2)
team's improvement must go to Joe Harris, the coach. To play as well as they do now, the coach
                                                                                    (3)
must have given the team superior instruction. There is no doubt that, if a coach is effective, his
influence is over many young minds.
                                                        (4)
     With this major victory behind them, the Tigers can now look forward to meet the
defending champions, the Revere Minutemen, in the finals.
                                        (5)
The win over the Cowboys was due to North Side's supremacy in the air. The Tigers'
                                                (6)
players have the advantages of strength and of being speedy. Our sterling quarterback, Butch
                                                        (7)
Carter, a master of the long pass, used these kind of passes to bedevil the boys from
                                                (8)
Western. As a matter of fact, if the Tigers would have used the passing offense earlier in the
game, the score would have been more one-sided. Butch, by the way, our all-around senior student, has already been tapped for bigger things. Having the highest marks in his class, Barton
                                (9)
College has offered him a scholarship.

     The team's defense is another story. During the last few weeks, neither the linebackers

(10)

nor the safety man <u>have shown</u> sufficient ability to contain their oppo nents' running game.

(11)

In the city final, <u>the defensive unit's failing to complete it's assignments</u> may lead to disaster.

(12)

However, the coach said that this unit <u>not only has been cooperative but also the coach raise</u>

(13)

<u>their eagerness to learn.</u> He also said that this team <u>has</u> not and <u>never will give up</u>.

(14)

This kind of spirit is contagious, <u>therefore</u> I predict that the Tigers will   win because I have

(15)

<u>affection and full confidence in</u> the team.

(16)

One of the happy surprises this season is Peter Yisko, our punter. Peter <u>is</u> in the United

States for only two years. When he was in grammar school in the old country, it was not nec-

(17)

essary for him <u>to have studied</u> hard. Now, he depends on the football team to help him with

(18)

his English. Everybody <u>but the team mascot and I have</u> been pressed into service. Peter was

(19)

ineligible last year when he <u>learned that he would only obtain half</u> of the credits he had com-

pleted in Europe. Nevertheless, he attended occasional practice sessions, but he soon found

(20)

out that, if one wants to be a success ful player, <u>you</u> must realize that regular practice is

(21)

required. In fact, if a team is to be successful, it is necessary that everyone <u>be</u> present for all

(22)

practice sessions. "The life of a football player," says Peter, "is better than <u>a scholar</u>."

Facing the Minutemen, the Tigers will meet their most formidable opposition yet. This

(23)

team <u>is not only gaining a bad reputation</u> but also indulging in illegal practices on the field.

(24)

They <u>can't hardly object to us being</u> technical about penalties under these circumstances.

(25)

As far as the Minutemen are concerned, a <u>victory will taste sweet like a victory should</u>.

1. A. that eliminated that team   1.____
    B. and they were eliminated
    C. and eliminated them
    D. Correct as is

2. A. To make them play as well as they do   2.____
    B. Having played so well
    C. After they played so well
    D. Correct as is

3. A. if coaches are effective; they have influence over   3.____
    B. to be effective, a coach influences
    C. if a coach is effective, he influences
    D. Correct as is

4. A. to meet with
    C. to a meeting of
    B. to meeting
    D. Correct as is
    4.____

5. A. because of
    C. motivated by
    B. on account of
    D. Correct as is
    5.____

6. A. operating swiftly
    C. running speedily
    B. speed
    D. Correct as is
    6.____

7. A. these kinds of pass
    C. this kind of pass
    B. this kind of passes
    D. Correct as is
    7.____

8. A. would of used
    C. were using
    B. had used
    D. Correct as is
    8.____

9. A. he was offered a scholarship by Barton College.
    B. Barton College offered a scholarship to him.
    C. a scholarship was offered him by Barton College.
    D. Correct as is
    9.____

10. A. had shown
    C. has shown
    B. were showing
    D. Correct as is
    10.____

11. A. the defensive unit failing to complete its assignment
    B. the defensive unit's failing to complete its assignment
    C. the defensive unit failing to complete it's assignment
    D. Correct as is
    11.____

12. A. has been not only cooperative, but also eager to learn
    B. has not only been cooperative, but also shows eagerness to learn
    C. has been not only cooperative, but also they were eager to learn
    D. Correct as is
    12.____

13. A. has not given up and never will
    B. has not and never would give up
    C. has not given up and never will give up
    D. Correct as is
    13.____

14. A. . Therefore
    C. -- therefore
    B. : therefore
    D. Correct as is
    14.____

15. A. full confidence and affection for
    B. affection for and full confidence in
    C. affection and full confidence concerning
    D. Correct as is
    15.____

16. A. is living
    C. has been
    B. was living
    D. Correct as is
    16.____

17. A. to study
    C. to have been studying
    B. to be studying
    D. Correct as is
    17.____

18.   A. but the team mascot and me has   18._____
         B. but the team mascot and myself has
         C. but the team mascot and me have
         D. Correct as is

19.   A. only learned that he would obtain half   19._____
         B. learned that he would obtain only half
         C. learned that he only would obtain half
         D. Correct as is

20.   A. a person   B. everyone   20._____
         C. one   D. one

21.   A. is   B. will be   21._____
         C. shall be   D. Correct as is

22.   A. to be a scholar   B. being a scholar   22._____
         C. that of a scholar   D. Correct as is

23.   A. not only is gaining a bad reputation   23._____
         B. is gaining not only a bad reputation
         C. is not gaining only a bad reputation
         D. Correct as is

24.   A. can hardly object to us being   24._____
         B. can hardly object to our being
         C. can't hardly object to our being
         D. Correct as is

25.   A. victory will taste sweet like it should   25._____
         B. victory will taste sweetly as it should taste
         C. victory will taste sweet as a victory should
         D. Correct as is

Questions 26-30.

DIRECTIONS: Questions 26 through 30 are to be answered on the basis of the instructions and paragraph which follow.

The paragraph which follows is part of a report prepared by a buyer for submission to his superior. The paragraph contains 5 underlined groups of words, each one bearing a number which identifies the question relating to it. Each of these groups of words MAY or MAY NOT represent standard written English, suitable for use in a formal report. For each question, decide whether the group of words used in the paragraph which is always choice A is standard written English and should be retained, or whether choice B, C, or D.

On October 23, 2009 the vendor delivered two microscopes to the using agency. <u>When</u>
   (26)
<u>they inspected</u>, one microscope was found to have a defective part. The vendor was notified,

and offered to replace the defective part; the using agency, however, requested <u>that the</u>
       (27)
<u>microscope be replaced</u>. The vendor claimed that complete replacement was unnecessary and

(28)

refused to comply with the agency's demand, <u>having the result that the agency declared</u> that it

(29)

will pay only for the acceptable microscope. At that point <u>I got involved by the agency's</u>

<u>contacting me</u>. The agency requested that I speak to the vendor since I handled the original

(30)

purchase and <u>have dealt with this vendor before</u>.

26.   A.   When they inspected,   26._____
            B.   Upon inspection,
            C.   The inspection report said that
            D.   Having inspected,

27.   A.   that the microscope be replaced.   27._____
            B.   a whole new microscope in replacement.
            C.   to have a replacement for the microscope.
            D.   that they get the microscope replaced.

28.   A.   , having the result that the agency declared   28._____
            B.   ; the agency consequently declared
            C.   , which refusal caused the agency to consequently declare
            D.   , with the result of the agency's declaring

29.   A.   I got involved by the agency's contacting me.   29._____
            B.   I became involved, being contacted by the agency.
            C.   the agency contacting me, I got involved.
            D.   the agency contacted me and I became involved.

30.   A.   have dealt with this vendor before.   30._____
            B.   done business before with this vendor.
            C.   know this vendor by prior dealings.
            D.   have dealt with this vendor before.

KEY (CORRECT ANSWERS)

1.	C	16.	C
2.	A	17.	A
3.	C	18.	A
4.	B	19.	B
5.	A	20.	C
6.	B	21.	D
7.	C	22.	C
8.	B	23.	D
9.	D	24.	A
10.	C	25.	C
11.	B	26.	B
12.	A	27.	A
13.	B	28.	B
14.	A	29.	D
15.	B	30.	D

ENGLISH GRAMMAR and USAGE

EXAMINATION SECTION
TEST 1

DIRECTIONS: In the passages that follow, certain words and phrases are underlined and numbered. In each question, you will find alternatives for each underlined part. You are to choose the one that BEST expresses the idea, makes the statement appropriate for standard written English, or is worded MOST consistently with the style and tone of the passage as a whole. Choose the alternative you consider BEST and write the letter in the space at the right. If you think the original version is BEST, choose NO CHANGE. Read each passage through once before you begin to answer the questions that accompany it. You cannot determine most answers without reading several sentences beyond the phrase in question. Be sure that you have read far enough ahead each time you choose an alternative.

Questions 1-14.

DIRECTIONS: Questions 1 through 14 are based on the following passage.

Modern filmmaking $\underline{\text{hadbegan}}$ in Paris in 1895 with the work of the Lumiere brothers.
1

Using their $\underline{\text{invention, the Cinématographe}}$ the Lumières were able to photograph, print,
2

and project moving pictures onto a screen. Their films showed $\underline{\text{actual occurrences.}}$ $\underline{\text{A}}$ train
3

approaching a station, people leaving a factory, workers demolishing a wall.

These early films had neither plot nor sound. But another Frenchman, Georges Méliès,

soon incorporated plot lines $\underline{\text{into}}$ his films. And with his attempts to draw upon the potential of
4

film to create fantasy $\underline{\text{worlds.}}$ Méliès also $\underline{\text{was an early pioneer from}}$ special film effects.
5 6

Edwin S. Porter, an American filmmaker, took Méliès's emphasis on narrative one step further.

Believing $\underline{\text{that, continuity of shots}}$ was of primary importance in filmmaking, Porter connected
7

$\underline{\text{images to present,}}$ a sustained action. His GREAT TRAIN ROBBERY of 1903 opened a new
8

era in film.

$\underline{\text{Because}}$ film was still considered $\underline{\text{as}}$ low entertainment in early twentieth century Amer-
9 10

ica, it was on its way to becoming a respected art form. Beginning in 1908, the American direc-

tor D.W. Griffith discovered and explored techniques to make film a more expressive

medium. With his technical contributions, <u>as well as</u> his attempts to develop the intellec-
                                          11
tual and moral potential of film, Griffith helped build a solid foundation for the industry.

   <u>Thirty</u> years after the Lumière brothers' first show, sound <u>had yet been</u> added to the
      12   13
movies. Finally, in 1927, Hollywood pro duced its first *talkie,* THE JAZZ SINGER. With sound,
modern film <u>coming</u> of age.
             14

1. A. NO CHANGE   1.____
    B. begun
    C. began
    D. had some beginnings

2. A. NO CHANGE   2.____
    B. hinvention - the Cinématogrape
    C. invention, the Cinématographe -
    D. invention, the Cinématographe

3. A. NO CHANGE   3.____
    B. actually occurrences, a
    C. actually occurrences - a
    D. actual occurrences: a

4. A. NO CHANGE   4.____
    B. about
    C. with
    D. to

5. A. NO CHANGE   5.____
    B. worlds,
    C. worlds; and
    D. worlds and

6. A. NO CHANGE   6.____
    B. pioneered
    C. pioneered the beginnings of
    D. pioneered the early beginnings of

7. A. NO CHANGE   7.____
    B. that continuity of shots
    C. that, continuity of shots,
    D. that continuity of shots

8. A. NO CHANGE   8.____
    B. images to present
    C. images and present
    D. images, and presenting

9.   A. NO CHANGE   9._____
        B. (Begin new paragraph) In view of the fact that
        C. (Begin new paragraph) Although
        D. (Do NOT begin new paragraph) Since

10.   A. NO CHANGE   10._____
        B. as if it were
        C. like it was
        D. OMIT the underlined portion

11.   A. NO CHANGE   11._____
        B. similar to
        C. similar with
        D. like with

12.   A. NO CHANGE   12._____
        B. (Begin new paragraph) Consequently, thirty
        C. (Do NOT begin new paragraph) Therefore, thirty
        D. (Do NOT begin new paragraph) As a consequence, thirty

13.   A. NO CHANGE   13._____
        B. had yet to be
        C. has yet
        D. was yet being

14.   A. NO CHANGE   14._____
        B. comes
        C. came
        D. had came

Questions 15-22.

DIRECTIONS: Questions 15 through 22 are based on the following passage.

    One of the most awesome forces in nature is the tsunami, or tidal wave. A

tsunami - the word is Japanese for harbor wave, can generate the destructive power of many
                  15

atomic bombs.

    Tsunamis usually appear in a series of four or five waves about fifteen minutes apart.
         16
They begin deep in the ocean, gather remarkable speed as they travel, and cover great distances. The wave triggered by the explosion of Krakatoa in 1883 circled the world in three days.

    Tsunamis being known to sink large ships at sea, they are most dangerous when they
       17

reach land. Close to shore, an oncoming tsunami is forced upward and skyward, perhaps
                                          18

as high as 100 feet. This combination of height and speed accounts for the tsunami's

great power.

That *tsunami* is a Japanese word is no accident, <u>due to the fact that</u> no nation
19

<u>frequently</u> has been so visited by giant waves as Japan. <u>Tsunamis</u> reach that country regu-
20   21
larly, and with devastating consequences. One Japanese tsunami flattened several towns in

<u>1896, also killed 27,000 people.</u> The 2011 tsunami caused similar loss of life as well as
22

untold damage from nuclear radiation.

15. A. NO CHANGE
    B. tsunami, the word is Japanese for harbor wave -
    C. tsunami - the word is Japanese for harbor wave -
    D. tsunami - the word being Japanese for harbor wave,

15.____

16. A. NO CHANGE
    B. (Begin new paragraph) Consequently, tsunamis
    C. (Do NOT begin new paragraph) Tsunamis consequently
    D. (Do NOT begin new paragraph) Yet, tsunamis

16.____

17. A. NO CHANGE
    B. Because tsunamis have been
    C. Although tsunamis have been
    D. Tsunamis have been

17.____

18. A. NO CHANGE
    B. upward to the sky,
    C. upward in the sky,
    D. upward,

18.____

19. A. NO CHANGE
    B. when one takes into consideration the fact that
    C. seeing as how
    D. for

19.____

20. A. NO CHANGE
    B. (Place after *has*)
    C. (Place after *so*)
    D. (Place after *visited*)

20.____

21. A. NO CHANGE
    B. Moreover, tsunamis
    C. However, tsunamis
    D. Because tsunamis

21.____

22. A. NO CHANGE
    B. 1896 and killed 27,000 people.
    C. 1896 and killing 27,000 people.
    D. 1896, and 27,000 people as well.

22.____

Questions 23-33.

DIRECTIONS: Questions 23 through 33 are based on the following passage.

I was $\underset{23}{\underline{\text{married one}}}$ August on a farm in Maine. The $\underset{24}{\underline{\text{ceremony, itself, taking}}}$ place in an

arbor of pine boughs $\underset{25}{\underline{\text{we had built and constructed}}}$ in the yard next to the house. On the

morning of the wedding day, we parked the tractors behind the shed, $\underset{26}{\underline{\text{have tied}}}$ the dogs to an

oak tree to keep them from chasing the guests, and put the cows out to pasture. $\underset{27}{\underline{\text{Thus}}}$ we had

thought of everything, it seemed. we had forgotten how interested a cow can be in what is going

on $\underset{28}{\underline{\text{around them.}}}$ During the ceremony, my sister $\underset{29}{\underline{\text{(who has taken several years of lessons)}}}$

was to play a flute solo. We were all listening intently when she $\underset{30}{\underline{\text{had began}}}$ to play. As the first

notes reached us, we were surprised to hear a bass line under the flute's treble melody. Looking

around, $\underset{31}{\underline{\text{the source was quicly discovered}}}$. There was Star, my pet Guernsey, her head hang-

ing over the pasture fence, mooing along with the delicate strains of Bach.

Star took our laughter $\underset{32}{\underline{\text{as being like}}}$ a compliment, and we took her contribution that way,

too. $\underset{33}{\underline{\text{It was}}}$ a sign of approval - the kind you would find only at a farm wedding.

23. A. NO CHANGE
    B. married, one
    C. married on an
    D. married, in an
              23._____

24. A. NO CHANGE
    B. ceremony itself taking
    C. ceremony itself took
    D. ceremony, itself took
              24._____

25. A. NO CHANGE
    B. which had been built and constructed
    C. we had built and constructed it
    D. we had built
              25._____

26. A. NO CHANGE
    B. tie
    C. tied
    D. tying
              26._____

27. A. NO CHANGE
    B. (Do NOT begin new paragraph) And
    C. (Begin new paragraph) But
    D. (Begin new paragraph) Moreover,
              27._____

28. A. NO CHANGE
    B. around her.
    C. in her own vicinity.
    D. in their immediate area.

28.____

29. A. NO CHANGE
    B. (whom has taken many years of lessons)
    C. (who has been trained in music)
    D. OMIT the underlined portion

29.____

30. A. NO CHANGE
    B. begun
    C. began
    D. would begin

30.____

31. A. NO CHANGE
    B. the discovery of the source was quick.
    C. the discovery of the source was quickly made.
    D. we quickly discovered the source.

31.____

32. A. NO CHANGE
    B. as
    C. just as
    D. as if

32.____

33. A. NO CHANGE
    B. Yet it was
    C. But it was
    D. Being

33.____

Questions 34-42.

DIRECTIONS: Questions 34 through 42 are based on the following passage.

Riding a bicycle in Great Britain is not the same as riding a bicycle in the United States. Americans bicycling in Britain will find some $\underset{34}{\underline{\text{basic fundamental}}}$ differences in the rules of the road and in the attitudes of motorists.

$\underset{35}{\underline{\text{Probably}}}$ most difficult for the American cyclist is adjusting $\underset{36}{\underline{\text{with}}}$ British traffic patterns.

$\underset{37}{\underline{\text{Knowing that traffic}}}$ in Britain moves on the left-hand side of the road, bicycling $\underset{38}{\underline{\text{once}}}$ there is the mirror image of what it is in the United States.

The problem of adjusting to traffic patterns is somewhat lessened, $\underset{39}{\underline{\text{however}}}$ by the respect with which British motorists treat bicyclists. A cyclist in a traffic circle, for example, is given the same right-of-way $\underset{40}{\underline{\text{with}}}$ the driver of any other vehicle. However, the cyclist is expected to obey

the rules of the road. This <u>difference in the American and British attitudes toward bicyclists</u>
41
may stem from differing attitudes toward the bicycle itself. Whereas Americans frequently view

bicycles as <u>toys, but</u> the British treat them primarily as vehicles.
42

34. A. NO CHANGE
    B. basic and fundamental
    C. basically fundamental
    D. basic

34.____

35. A. NO CHANGE
    B. Even so, probably
    C. Therefore, probably
    D. As a result, probably

35.____

36. A. NO CHANGE
    B. upon
    C. on
    D. to

36.____

37. A. NO CHANGE
    B. Seeing that traffic
    C. Because traffic
    D. Traffic

37.____

38. A. NO CHANGE
    B. once you are
    C. once one is
    D. OMIT the underlined portion

38.____

39. A. NO CHANGE
    B. also,
    C. moreover,
    D. therefore,

39.____

40. A. NO CHANGE
    B. as
    C. as if
    D. as with

40.____

41. A. NO CHANGE
    B. difference in the American and British attitudes toward bicyclists
    C. difference, in the American and British attitudes toward bicyclists
    D. difference in the American, and British, attitudes toward bicyclists

41.____

42. A. NO CHANGE
    B. toys;
    C. toys,
    D. toys; but

42.____

Questions 43-51.

DIRECTIONS: Questions 43 through 51 are based on the following passage.

People have always believed that supernatural powers <u>tend toward some influence on</u>
43

lives for good or for ill. Superstition originated with the idea that individuals <u>could in turn,</u> exert
44

influence <u>at</u> spirits. Certain superstitions are <u>so deeply embedded</u> in our culture that intelli-
45   46
gent people sometimes act in accordance with them.

One common superstitious act is knocking on wood after boasting of good fortune. People once believed that gods inhabited trees and, therefore, were present in the wood used to build houses. Fearing that speaking of good luck within the gods' hearing might anger

<u>them, people</u> knocked on wood to deafen the gods and avoid their displeasure.
47

Another superstitious <u>custom and practice</u> is throwing salt over the left shoulder.
48

<u>Considering</u> salt was once considered sacred, people thought that spilling it brought bad luck.
49
Since right and left represented good and evil, the believers used their right hands, which symbolized good, to throw a pinch of salt over their left shoulders into the eyes of the evil gods.

<u>Because of this,</u> people attempted to avert misfortune.
50

Without realizing the origin of superstitions, many people exhibit superstitious behavior.

<u>Others avoid</u> walking under ladders and stepping on cracks in sidewalks, without having any
51
idea why they are doing so.

43. A. NO CHANGE
    B. can influence
    C. tend to influence on
    D. are having some influence on

44. A. NO CHANGE
    B. could, turning,
    C. could, in turn,
    D. could, in turn

45. A. NO CHANGE
    B. of
    C. toward
    D. on

46. A. NO CHANGE
    B. so deep embedded
    C. deepest embedded
    D. embedded deepest

46.____

47. A. NO CHANGE
    B. them; people
    C. them: some people
    D. them, they

47.____

48. A. NO CHANGE
    B. custom
    C. traditional custom
    D. customary habit

48.____

49. A. NO CHANGE
    B. Although
    C. Because
    D. Keeping in mind that

49.____

50. A. NO CHANGE
    B. As a result of this,
    C. Consequently,
    D. In this way,

50.____

51. A. NO CHANGE
    B. Often avoiding
    C. Avoiding
    D. They avoid

51.____

Questions 52-66.

DIRECTIONS: Questions 52 through 66 are based on the following passage.

In the 1920s, the Y.M.C.A. sponsored one of the first programs <u>in order to promote</u> more
52

enlightened public opinion on racial matters; the organization started special university classes

<u>in which</u> young people could study race relations. Among the guest speakers invited to conduct
53

the sessions, one of the most popular was George Washington Carver, the scientist from Tuske-
gee Institute.

As a student, Carver himself had been active in the Y.M.C.A. <u>He shared</u> its evangelical
54

and educational philosophy. However, in <u>1923,</u> the Y.M.C.A. arranged <u>Carver's first initial</u>
55   56

speaking tour, the scientist accepted with apprehension. He was to speak at several white col-
leges, most of whose students had never seen, let alone heard, an educated black man.

Although Carver's appearances <u>did sometimes</u> cause occasional <u>controversy, but</u> his
57 58
quiet dedication prevailed, and his humor quickly won over his audiences. <u>Nevertheless, for</u>
59
the next decade, Carver toured the Northeast, Midwest, and South under Y.M.C.A.

<u>sponsorship. Speaking</u> at places never before open to blacks. On these tours Carver
60

befriended thousands of students, many of <u>whom</u> subsequently corresponded with
61

his <u>afterwards.</u> The <u>tours, unfortunately were</u> not without discomfort for Carver. There were
62 63

the indignities of *Jim Crow* accommodations and racial insults from strangers. <u>As a result,</u> the
64

scientist's enthusiasm never faltered. <u>Avoiding any discussion of</u> the political and social
65

aspects of racial injustice; instead, Carver conducted his whole life as an indirect attack <u>to</u>
66
prejudice. This, as much as his science, is his legacy to humankind.

52.
A. NO CHANGE
B. to promote
C. for the promoting of what is
D. for the promotion of what are
52._____

53.
A. NO CHANGE
B. from which
C. that
D. by which
53._____

54.
A. No Change
B. Sharing
C. Having Shared
D. Because He Shared
54._____

55.
A. NO CHANGE
B. 1923
C. 1923, and
D. 1923, when
55._____

56.
A. NO CHANGE
B. Carvers' first, initial
C. Carvers first initial
D. Carver's first
56._____

57.
   A. NO CHANGE
   B. sometimes did
   C. did
   D. OMIT the underlined portion

57._____

58.
   A. NO CHANGE
   B. controversy and
   C. controversy,
   D. controversy, however

58._____

59.
   A. NO CHANGE
   B. However, for
   C. However, from
   D. For

59._____

60.
   A. NO CHANGE
   B. sponsorship and spoke
   C. sponsorship; and spoke
   D. sponsorship, and speaking

60._____

61.
   A. NO CHANGE
   B. who
   C. them
   D. those

61._____

62.
   A. NO CHANGE
   B. later.
   C. sometime later.
   D. OMIT the underlined portion and end the sentence with a period

62._____

63.
   A. NO CHANGE
   B. tours, unfortunately, were
   C. tours unfortunately, were
   D. tours, unfortunately, are

63._____

64.
   A. NO CHANGE
   B. So
   C. But
   D. Therefore,

64._____

65.
   A. NO CHANGE
   B. He avoided discussing
   C. Having avoided discussing
   D. Upon avoiding the discussion of

65._____

66.
   A. NO CHANGE
   B. over
   C. on
   D. of

66._____

Questions 67-75.

DIRECTIONS: Questions 67 through 75 are based on the following passage.

Shooting rapids is not the only way to experience the thrill of canoeing. $\underset{67}{\underline{An}}$ ordinary-looking stream, innocent of rocks and white water, can provide adventure, as long as it has three essential $\underset{68}{\underline{features;}}$ a swift current, close banks, and $\underset{69}{\underline{has}}$ plenty of twists and turns.

$\underset{70}{\underline{A}}$ powerful current causes tension, for canoeists know they will have only seconds for executing the maneuvers necessary to prevent crashing into the trees lining the narrow $\underset{71}{\underline{streams\ banks.}}$ Of course, the $\underset{72}{\underline{narrowness,\ itself,\ being}}$ crucial in creating the tension. On a broad stream, canoeists can pause frequently, catch their breath, and get their bearings. However, $\underset{73}{\underline{to}}$ a narrow stream, where every minute $\underset{74}{\underline{you\ run}}$ the risk of being knocked down by a low-hanging tree limb, they must be constantly alert. Yet even the fast current and close banks would be manageable if the stream were fairly straight. The expenditure of energy required to paddle furiously, first on one side of the canoe and then on the other, wearies $\underset{75}{\underline{both\ the\ nerves\ as\ well\ as\ the\ body.}}$

67.
A. NO CHANGE
B. They say that for adventure an
C. Many finding that an
D. The old saying that an

67.____

68.
A. NO CHANGE
B. features:
C. features,
D. features; these being

68.____

69.
A. NO CHANGE
B. there must be
C. with
D. OMIT the underlined portion

69.____

70.
A. NO CHANGE
B. Thus, a
C. Therefore, a
D. Furthermore, a

70.____

71.
A. NO CHANGE
B. stream's banks.
C. streams bank's.
D. banks of the streams.

71.____

72.
A. NO CHANGE
B. narrowness, itself is
C. narrowness itself is
D. narrowness in itself being

72.____

73. A. NO CHANGE
    B. near
    C. on
    D. with

73.____

74. A. NO CHANGE
    B. the canoer runs
    C. one runs
    D. they run

74.____

75. A. NO CHANGE
    B. the nerves as well as the body
    C. the nerves, also, as well as the body
    D. not only the body but also the nerves as well

75.____

KEY (CORRECT ANSWERS)

1.	C	26.	C	51.	D
2.	A	27.	C	52.	B
3.	D	28.	B	53.	A
4.	A	29.	D	54.	A
5.	B	30.	C	55.	D
6.	B	31.	D	56.	D
7.	D	32.	B	57.	C
8.	B	33.	A	58.	C
9.	C	34.	D	59.	D
10.	D	35.	A	60.	B
11.	A	36.	D	61.	A
12.	A	37.	C	62.	D
13.	B	38.	D	63.	B
14.	C	39.	A	64.	C
15.	C	40.	B	65.	B
16.	A	41.	A	66.	C
17.	C	42.	C	67.	A
18.	D	43.	B	68.	B
19.	D	44.	C	69.	D
20.	C	45.	D	70.	A
21.	A	46.	A	71.	B
22.	B	47.	A	72.	C
23.	A	48.	B	73.	C
24.	C	49.	C	74.	D
25.	D	50.	D	75.	B

EXAMINATION SECTION
TEST 1

DIRECTIONS: In the following questions, you are given a complete sentence which you are to rewrite in your mind, starting with the words given just below it. Make whatever changes the new sentence plan requires, but no others; do not change the overall meaning of the sentence. (Note that you are not correcting a mistake in the original sentence; you are simply changing the construction. The revised sentence should be grammatically correct, but it need not necessarily be a better way of expressing the meaning. There may be more than one way of recasting the sentence but only one will enable you to answer the question.) Read the directions for each question carefully. They may specify that the missing word or expression appear somewhere in the rewritten sentence; they may ask for the next word in the rewritten sentence, the word following a specific word, etc. *PRINT THE LETTER OF THE CORRECT ANSWER IN THE SPACE AT THE RIGHT.*

1. *As a literary genre, the messianic drama falls into the category of myth or romance, for its central figure conforms to the definitions supplied by Northrup Frye, in THE ANATOMY OF CRITICISM, of the mythic hero.*
   REWRITTEN:
   Because its central figure conforms to the definitions of the mythic hero supplied by Northrup Frye, in THE ANATOMY OF CRITICISM, the messianic drama is….

   The NEXT WORD in the rewritten sentence is
   A. into   B. literary   C. categorized
   D. categorically   E. a

   1.____

2. *In THE EMPEROR JULIAN, the second part of the drama, Ibsen reveals Julian to be a false Messiah.*
   REWRITTEN:
   Julian is….

   Somewhere in the part of the rewritten sentence indicated by dots is the word
   A. reveals   B. by   C. falsified
   D. in which   E. messianic

   2.____

3. *More interesting, because more subtly hidden, is Chekhov's use of melodrama.*
   REWRITTEN:
   Because it is more….

   The NEXT WORD in the rewritten sentence is
   A. subtly   B. interesting   C. melodramatic
   D. used   E. hidden

   3.____

4. *Shaw's response to this is to withdraw, partially, from his pubic concerns into a more personal, private, and poetic form of expression.*
   REWRITTEN:
   Shaw responded to this with a ....

   Somewhere in the part of the rewritten sentence indicated by dots is the word
   A. partially   B. is to   C. withdraws
   D. publicly   E withdrawal

   4.____

5. *But life draws him back again, against his will, in the form of uncontrollable instinct.*
   REWRITTEN:
   He is....

   The MEXT WORD in the rewritten sentence is
   A. uncontrollable   B. instinctive   C. back
   D. drawn   E. willful

   5.____

6. *Such destructive criticism accounts, in part, for the unpopularity of this drama, for the modern world wants affirmations.*
   REWRITTEN:
   This drama is

   The NEXT WORD in the rewritten sentence is
   A. unpopular   B. accounted   C. criticized
   D. in part   E. destructive

   6.____

7. *Shaw is just as unable to accept the concept of a malevolent or determined man as to accept the concept of a determined and mindless universe.*
   REWRITTEN:
   It is equally difficult....

   Somewhere in the part of the rewritten sentence indicated by dots is(are) the word(s)
   A. unable   B. for him   C. just
   D. to conceive   E. to understand

   7.____

8. *We know from his descriptions that Leeuwenhoek saw both plant and animal microorganisms and that among them may have been some bacteria.*
   REWRITTEN:
   Among the plant and animal microorganisms which we....

   The MEXT WORD in the rewritten sentence is
   A. saw   B. described   C. know
   D. assume   E. discovered

   8.____

9. *The Japanese quickly overcame the Russian fleet and then landed troops on the mainland of Asia.*
   REWRITTEN:
   The Russian fleet....

   Somewhere in the part of the rewritten sentence indicated by dots is(are) the word(s)

   A. overcame   B. and then   C. defeated
   D. retreated   E. who

   9.____

10. *Napoleon would not tolerate such an arrangement and sent an army of twenty thousand men to suppress the movement.*
    REWRITTEN:
    The movement....

    The NEXT WORD in the rewritten sentence is

    A. was   B. suppressed   C. would
    D. sent   E. of

    10.____

11. *To have the program succeed, Marx realized he would need the united support of workingmen all over the world.*
    REWRITTEN:
    Marx realized that the success....

    Somewhere in the part of the rewritten sentence indicated by dots is the word

    A. he   B. would   C. have   D. required   E. to

    11.____

12. *His beautiful descriptions of nature reflect the poet's deep belief in the closeness of nature to the human soul.*
    REWRITTEN:
    One reflection of....

    The NEXT WORD(S) in the rewritten sentence is(are)

    A. beauty   B. the poet's   C. poetry
    D. the descriptions   E. closeness

    12.____

13. *The extraordinary play is a chronicle of O'Neill's own spiritual metamorphosis from a messianic into an existential rebel.*
    REWRITTEN:
    O'Neill had undergone....

    The NEXT WORD in the rewritten sentence is

    A. extraordinary   B. existentialism   C. rebelliousness
    D. spirituality   E. a

    13.____

14. *Considering its great influence, Europe is surprisingly small.*
    REWRITTEN:
    The smallness of Europe is surprising when one....

    14.____

The NEXT WORD in the rewritten sentence is
A. influences   B. is   C. considers
D. knows   E. consideration

15. *Until late in the 1800's we knew nothing of a remarkable civilization which was old when the Greeks arrived.*
REWRITTEN:
One remarkable civilization which was old when the Greeks arrived....

    15.____

Somewhere in the part of the rewritten sentence indicated by dots if the word
A. we   B. unknown   C. knew
D. nothing   E. of

16. *Our knowledge of Aegean civilization comes largely from the work of two men.*
REWRITTEN:
The work of two men....

    16.____

The NEXT WORD in the rewritten sentence is
A. comes   B. teaches   C. acknowledges
D. enhances   E. contributes

17. *Twelve of the most important deities formed a council, which was supposed to meet on snowcapped Mount Olympus, in northern Thessaly.*
REWRITTEN:
Mount Olympus, in northern Thessaly, was supposed to be the....

    17.____

The NEXT WORD(S) in the rewritten sentence is(are)
A. meeting place   B. council   C. most important
D. epitome   E. deities'

18. *In the United States the states and local governments regulate the public schools and supply them with funds.*
REWRITTEN:
Public schools in the United States are....

    18.____

Somewhere in the part of the rewritten sentence indicated by dots is the word
A. them   B. regulate   C. subsidized
D. governed   E. supplied

19. *The obstacle of distance was partly overcome by the invention of the steamship and the building of the Suez Canal.*
REWRITTEN:
The invention of the steamship and the building of the Suez Canal helped....

    19.____

Somewhere in the part of the rewritten sentence indicated by dots is the word
A. was   B. overcoming   C. overcome
D. partly   E. shorten

20. *Although cotton has been used for cloth since ancient times, it was not known in England until the seventeenth century when the East India Company brought "calico" (named for Calicut) from India.*
REWRITTEN:
When the East India Company brought "calico" (named for Calicut) from India in the seventeenth century, it was England's first....

Somewhere in the part of the rewritten sentence indicated by dots is the word
   A. known   B. knowledge   C. was
   D. although   E. until

20.____

21. *In the eighteenth century weaving was still done on the hand loom.*
REWRITTEN:
The hand loom....

Somewhere in the part of the rewritten sentence indicated by dots is the word
   A. done   B. on   C. for
   D. remained   E. weaves

21.____

22. *When rubbed with wool, amber accumulates a charge of static electricity and will then attract small pieces of pith or paper.*
REWRITTEN:
Small pieces of pith or paper can....

The NEXT WORD in the rewritten sentence is
   A. accumulate   B. be   C. attract
   D. charge   E. then

22.____

23. *As a result of the Second World War, cities were devastated and millions were left homeless.*
REWRITTEN:
The Second World War resulted....

Somewhere in the part of the rewritten sentence indicated by dots is(are) the word(s)
   A. leaving   B. devastating   C. were
   D. deprivation   E. devastated

23.____

24. *With the growing urbanization and mechanization of modern life has come* increasing recognition of the evils of drunkenness.
REWRITTEN:
The evils of drunkenness have become....

Somewhere in the part of the rewritten sentence indicated by dots is the word
   A. recognition   B. recognized   C. come
   D. increasing   E. increased

24.____

25. *Chekhov dilutes the melodramatic pathos by qualifying our sympathy for the victims.*
REWRITTEN:
The result of Chekhov's....

The NEXT WORD in the rewritten sentence is
A. dilution
B. diluting
C. melodramatic
D. qualification
E. qualifying

25.____

KEY (CORRECT ANSWERS)

1.	C		11.	D
2.	B		12.	B
3.	A		13.	E
4.	E		14.	C
5.	D		15.	B
6.	A		16.	E
7.	B		17.	A
8.	C		18.	E
9.	E		19.	C
10.	A		20.	D

21.	C
22.	B
23.	A
24.	B
25.	E

SOLUTIONS TO PROBLEMS

1. Because its central figure conforms to the definitions of the mythic hero supplied by Northrup Frye, in THE ANATOMY OF CRITICISM, the messianic drama is <u>categorized</u> in the literary genre of myth or romance.

2. Julian is revealed <u>by</u> Ibsen to be a false Messiah, in THE EMPEROR JULIAN, the second part of the drama.

3. Because it is more <u>subtly</u> hidden, Chekhov's use of melodrama is more interesting.

4. Shaw responded to this with a partial <u>withdrawal</u> from his public concerns into a more personal, private, and poetic form of expression.

5. He is <u>drawn</u> back again by life, against his will, in the form of uncontrollable instinct.

6. This drama is <u>unpopular</u> partly because it receives such destructive criticism when the modern world wants affirmations.

7. It is equally difficult for Shaw to accept the concept of a malevolent or determined man as it is <u>for him</u> to accept the concept of a determined and mindless universe.

8. Among the plant and animal microorganisms which we <u>know</u> that Leeuwenhoek saw because of his descriptions, there may have been some bacteria.

9. The Russian fleet was quickly overcome by the Japanese <u>who</u> then landed troops on the mainland of Asia.

10. The movement <u>was</u> suppressed by an army of twenty thousand men sent by Napoleon who would not tolerate such an arrangement.

11. Marx realized that the success of the program <u>required</u> the united support of workingmen all over the world

12. One reflection of <u>the poet's</u> deep belief in the closeness of nature to the human soul can be found in his beautiful descriptions of nature.

13. O'Neill had undergone <u>a</u> spiritual metamorphosis from a messianic into an existential rebel, of which this play is an extraordinary chronicle.

14. The smallness of Europe is surprising when one <u>considers</u> its great influence.

15. One remarkable civilization which was old when the Greeks arrived was <u>unknown</u> to us until late in the 1800's.

16. The work of two men <u>contributes</u> largely to our knowledge of Aegean civilization.

17. Snowcapped Mount Olympus, in northern Thessaly, was supposed to be the <u>meeting place</u> for a council formed by twelve of its most important deities.

18. Public schools in the United States are regulated and <u>supplied</u> with funds by the states and local government.

19. The invention of the steamship and the building of the Suez Canal helped to <u>overcome</u> the obstacle of distance.

20. When the East India Company brought "calico" (named for Calicut) from India in the seventeenth century, it was England's first introduction to cotton, <u>although</u> it has been used for cloth since ancient times.

21. The hand loom was still used <u>for</u> weaving in the eighteenth century.

22. Small pieces of pith or paper <u>can</u> be attracted by amber if it has been rubbed into wool to accumulate a charge of static electricity.

23. The Second World War resulted in the devastation of cities and the <u>leaving</u> homeless of millions.

24. The evils of drunkenness have become increasingly <u>recognized</u> with the growing urbanization and mechanization of modern life.

25. The result of Chekhov's <u>qualifying</u> our sympathy for the victims if the dilution of the melodramatic pathos.

————————

TEST 2

DIRECTIONS: In the following questions, you are given a complete sentence which you are to rewrite in your mind, starting with the words given just below it. Make whatever changes the new sentence plan requires, but no others; do not change the overall meaning of the sentence. (Note that you are not correcting a mistake in the original sentence; you are simply changing the construction. The revised sentence should be grammatically correct, but it need not necessarily be a better way of expressing the meaning. There may be more than one way of recasting the sentence but only one will enable you to answer the question.) Read the directions for each question carefully. They may specify that the missing word or expression appear somewhere in the rewritten sentence; they may ask for the next word in the rewritten sentence, the word following a specific word, etc. *PRINT THE LETTER OF THE CORRECT ANSWER IN THE SPACE AT THE RIGHT.*

1.   *While gazing through his microscope at a drop of water, he saw many kinds of*   1.____
     of creatures with one or a few cells, which wriggled about and devoured food.
     BEGIN THE SENTENCE WITH:
     Many kinds of creatures with one or a few cells wriggling about….

     Somewhere in the part of the rewritten sentence indicated by dots is(are) the
     word(s)
        A. he saw   B. and devoured   C. which
        D. by him   E. while gazing

2.   *The worship of ancestors in China must have arisen in prehistoric times,*   2.____
     judging from the references to it in the most ancient Chinese literature.
     SUBSTITUTE:
     …since the most ancient Chinese literature for judging

     The NEXT WORDS in the rewritten sentence are
        A. the references   B. is judged   C. refers it
        D. refers to   E. from the

3.   *She divided the bread among them, without considering a share for herself.*   3.____
     BEGIN THE SENTENCE WITH:
     She did not….

     Somewhere in the part of the rewritten sentence indicated by dots is(are) the
     word(s)
        A. divided   B. when she   C. without
        D. considering   E. dividing

4.   *Since Smith has been a resident here for twenty years, we should give serious*   4.____
     consideration to his suggestions.
     SUBSTITUTE:
     …seriously for give serious

The NEXT WORD(S) in the rewritten sentence is(are)
A. to B. consideration C. consider
D. give consideration E. would

5. *In the fight for women's suffrage, one judge's decision had little effect, for the most part, upon the ladies' determination.*
CHANGE:
effect to effected

Somewhere in the part of the rewritten sentence indicated by dots is(are) the word(s)
A. had B. upon C. part, upon
D. had, for E. part, very little

5._____

6. *His approach to the committee was certainly not conducive to a cordial reception of his proposals, which were, at best, of doubtful validity.*
BEGIN THE SENTENCE WITH:
He approached….

Somewhere in the part of the rewritten sentence indicated by dots is(are) the word(s)
A. was certainly B. which was C. to the
D. his E. committee was

6._____

7. *When the thirsty horse had drunk its fill, it trotted briskly down the road.*
BEGIN THE SENTENCE WITH:
The thirsty horse….

The NEXT WORD(S) in the rewritten sentence is(are)
A. having B. it trotted C. when
D. had E. had trotted

7._____

8. *This country must either set up flood controls or be prepared to lose billions of dollars annually.*
BEGIN THE SENTENCE WITH:
If….

Somewhere in the part of the rewritten sentence indicated by dots is(are) the word(s)
A. either B. must set C. does not
D. or E. country must

8._____

9. *They are not in Boston now, but I think they're going to that city next week.*
BEGIN THE SENTENCE WITH:
I think….

9._____

Somewhere in the part of the rewritten sentence indicated by dots is(are) the word(s)

   A. but I   B. in Boston   C. to Boston
   D. to that   E. now, but

10. *Mt. Kinley, in Alaska, is higher than any other mountain in North America.*   10.____
     INSERT THE WORD:
     <u>the</u> after <u>is</u>....

     The NEXT WORD in the rewritten sentence is
        A. highest   B. other   C. any
        D. than   E. higher

11. *As a result of the Industrial Revolution, cities grew very rapidly and the demand*   11.____
     for food and raw materials increased.
     BEGIN THE SENTENCE WITH:
     A result....

     Somewhere in the part of the rewritten sentence indicated by dots is(are) the word(s)

        A. grew   B. rapidly   C. the demand
        D. materials increased   E. increased demand

12. *Since the late eighteenth century, when the American and French revolutions*   12.____
     took place, democracy has had a slow but persistent growth.
     SUBSTITUTE:
     <u>After</u> for <u>Since</u>....

     Somewhere in the part of the rewritten sentence indicated by dots is(are) the] word(s)

        A. slow   B. has had   C. persistently
        D. growth   E. slow but persistent

13. *The Treaty of Versailles placed the entire blame for World War I on Germany*   13.____
     and her allies.
     BEGIN THE SENTENCE WITH:
     Germany....

     Somewhere in the part of the rewritten sentence indicated by dots is the word

        A. placed   B. on   C. blame   D. were   E. entire

14. *A few years after Harvey's death, other scientists began to study the blood*   14.____
     vessels with the aid of microscopes.
     BEGIN THE SENTENCE WITH:
     Blood vessels....

     Somewhere in the part of the rewritten sentence indicated by dots is(are) the word(s)

        A. by   B. began   C. study   D. to   E. the study

15. *This pamphlet is in response to requests of various groups for a more permanent and usable form of this material.*
BEGIN THE SENTENCE WITH:
To provide….

15.____

Somewhere in the part of the rewritten sentence indicated by dots is(are) the word(s)
- A. responding to
- B. as a response to
- C. requested
- D. in response to
- E. requesting

16. *The space science events chosen for development illustrate types of experiences in which mathematics and science have a mutually enhancing effect on each other.*
SUBSTITUTE:
….<u>are illustrated by</u> for <u>illustrate</u>

16.____

Somewhere in the part of the rewritten sentence indicated by dots is(are) the word(s)
- A. have had
- B. have
- C. had had
- D. may be shown to have
- E. has

17. *The criteria will be useful throughout the course in setting up specific objectives, providing learning experiences, and making periodic evaluations.*
SUBSTITUTE:
<u>course</u>….

17.____

The NEXT WORD in the rewritten sentence is
- A. in
- B. for
- C. to
- D. with
- E. by

18. *The objectives of a training program are achieved by learning experiences designed to help the trainees develop those behaviors and abilities designated in the objectives.*
BEGIN THE SENTENCE WITH:
To achieve….

18.____

Somewhere in the part of the rewritten sentence indicated by dots is(are) the word(s)
- A. employ
- B. to use
- C. it will be useful
- D. create
- E. to create

19. *Because all of the suggested facilities will not be available in every community, it remains for the teacher to modify or supplement the following suggestions.*
BEGIN THE SENTENCE WITH:
The teacher….

19.____

The word that occurs immediately before the word *modify* is
- A. could
- B. might
- C. would
- D. must
- E. should

20. *Although teachers differ in their ways of organizing and coordinating important parts of their presentations, they agree that the purpose of a lesson is effective and meaningful classroom instruction.*
BEGIN THE SENTENCE WITH:
Although teachers agree....

20.____

The FIRST WORD of the main clause in the rewritten sentence is
   A. the   B. teachers   C. they   D. differing   E. it

21. *Many common physical quantities such as temperature, the speed of a moving object, or the displacement of a ship can be expressed as a certain number of units.*
BEGIN THE SENTENCE WITH:
One can express....

21.____

The NEXT WORD(S) in the rewritten sentence is(are)
   A. as   B. many   C. in   D. a ship's   E. the

22. *A parallel-tuned circuit, on the other hand, offers a very high impedance to currents of its natural, or resonant, frequency and a relatively low impedance to others.*
BEGIN THE SENTENCE WITH:
A very high impedance....

22.____

The NEXT WORDS in the rewritten sentence are
   A. is offered to   B. others to   C. is offered for
   D. is offered by   E. on the other hand

23. *As the term implies, a voltage feedback amplifier transfers a voltage from the output of the amplifier back to its input.*
CHANGE:
....transfers to is transferred

23.____

The FIRST WORDS of the rewritten sentence are
   A. A voltage   B. Back to its input
   C. A voltage feedback amplifier D. In accordance with the term
   E. From the output

24. *Unemployment among youth is a serious problem now, and unless the economy grows much more rapidly in the future than it has during the past decade, today's youngsters will feel the sharp pinch of declining ratios of new employment opportunities to persons seeking work.*
BEGIN THE SENTENCE WITH:
Unless the economy grows, ...

24.____

The LAST CLAUSE in the rewritten sentence begins with
   A. today's   B. unemployment   C. and unless
   D. now   E. since

131

25. *In a great society, talents are evoked and realized, creative minds probe the frontiers of knowledge, expectations of excellence are widely shared.*
BEGIN THE SENTENCE WITH:
A great society....

25.____

The NEXT WORDS in the rewritten sentence are
   A. evokes and realizes
   B. talents, creative minds, and expectations of excellence
   C. features
   D. is characterized by
   E. in one in which

KEY (CORRECT ANSWERS)

1.	D		11.	E
2.	D		12.	C
3.	B		13.	D
4.	C		14.	A
5.	E		15.	D
6.	B		16.	B
7.	A		17.	C
8.	C		18.	A
9.	C		19.	E
10.	A		20.	C

21.	A
22.	E
23.	A
24.	E
25.	E

SOLUTIONS TO PROBLEMS

1. Many kinds of creatures with one or a few cells, wriggling about and devouring food, were seen <u>by him</u> while he was gazing through his microscope at a drop of water.

2. The worship of ancestors in China must have arisen in prehistoric times since the most ancient Chinese literature <u>refers to</u> it.

3. She did not consider a share for herself <u>when she</u> divided the bread among them.

4. Since Smith has been a resident here for twenty years, we should seriously <u>consider</u> his suggestions.

5. In the fight for women's suffrage, one judge's decision affected the ladies' decision, for the most <u>part, very little</u>.

6. He approached the community in a way <u>which was</u> certainly not conducive to a cordial reception of his proposals, which were, at best, of doubtful validity.

7. The thirsty horse, having drunk its fill, trotted briskly down the road.

8. If this country <u>does not</u> set up flood controls, it must be prepared to lose billions of dollars annually.

9. I think they're going <u>to Boston</u> next week, though they're not in that city now.

10. Mr. Kinley, in Alaska, is the <u>highest</u> mountain in North America.

11. A result of the Industrial Revolution was the very rapid growth of cities and the <u>increased demand</u> for food and raw materials.

12. After the late eighteenth century, when the American and French revolutions took place, democracy grew slowly, but <u>persistently</u>.

13. Germany and her allies <u>were</u> blamed entirely for World War I by the Treaty of Versailles.

14. Blood vessels were studied <u>by</u> other scientists, with the aid of microscopes, a few years after Harvey's death.

15. To provide a more permanent and usable form of this material, <u>in response to</u> the requests of various groups, this pamphlet has been written.

16. The space scientist events chosen for development are illustrated by types of experiences in which mathematics and science <u>have</u> a mutually enhancing effect on each other.

17. Use the criteria throughout the course <u>to</u> set up specific objectives, provide learning experiences, and make periodic evaluations.

18. To achieve the objectives of a training program, <u>employ</u> learning experiences designed to help the trainees develop those behaviors and abilities designated in the objectives.

19. The teacher <u>should</u> modify or supplement the following suggestions because all of the suggested facilities will not be available in every community.

20. Although teachers agree that the purpose of a lesson is effective and meaningful classroom instruction, <u>they</u> differ in their ways of organizing and coordinating important parts of their presentations.]

21. One can express <u>as</u> a certain number of units many common physical quantities such as temperature, the speed of a moving object, or the displacement of a ship.

22. A very high impedance, <u>on the other hand</u>, is offered by a parallel-tuned circuit to currents of its natural, or resonant, frequency and a relatively low impedance to others.

23. <u>A voltage</u> is transferred from the output of the amplifier back to its input by a voltage feedback amplifier, as its name implies.

24. Unless the economy grows much more rapidly in the future than it has during the past decade, today's youngsters will feel the sharp pinch of declining ratios of new employment opportunities to persons seeking work <u>since</u> unemployment among youth is a serious problem now.

25. A great society <u>is one in which</u> talents are evoked and realized, creative minds probe the frontiers of knowledge, expectations of excellence are widely shared.

———

BASIC FUNDAMENTALS OF WRITTEN COMMUNICATION

CONTENTS   Page

BASIC FUNDAMENTALS OF WRITTEN COMMUNICATION

INSTRUCTIONAL OBJECTIVES

1. Ability to write legibly.
2. Ability to fill out forms and applications correctly.
3. Ability to take messages and notes accurately.
4. Ability to write letters effectively.
5. Ability to write directions and instructions clearly.
6. Ability to outline written and spoken information.
7. Ability to persuade or teach others through written communication.
8. Ability to write effective overviews and summaries.
9. Ability to make smooth transitions within written communications.
10. Ability to use language forms appropriate for the reader.
11. Ability to prepare effective informational reports.

CONTENT

INTRODUCTION

Public-service employees are required to prepare written communications for a variety of purposes. Written communication is a fundamental tool, not only for the public-service occupations, but throughout the world of work. Many public-service occupations require written communication with ordinary citizens of diverse backgrounds, so the trainee should develop the ability to write in simple, nontechnical language that the ordinary citizen will understand.

This unit is designed to develop the student's ability to communicate effectively in writing for a number of different purposes and in a number of different formats. Whatever the particular purpose or format, how·· ever, effective writing will require the writer:

- to have a clear idea of his purpose and his audience;
- to organize his thoughts and information in an orderly way;
- to express himself concisely, accurately, and concretely;
- to report relevant facts;
- to explain and summarize ideas clearly; and
- to evaluate the effectiveness of his communication.

1. **BUSINESS WRITING**

Several forms of written communication tend to recur frequently in most public-service agencies, including:

- letters
- forms
- memoranda
- minutes of meetings
- short reports
- telegrams and cables
- news releases
- and many others

The public-service employee should be familiar with the principles of writing in these forms, and should be able to apply them in preparing effective communications.

Letters

Every letter sent from a public-service agency should be considered an ambassador of goodwill. The impression it creates may mean the difference between favorable public attitudes or unfavorable ones. It may mean the difference between creating a friend or an enemy for the agency. Every public-service employee has a responsibility to serve the public effectively and to provide services in an efficient and courteous manner. The letters an agency sends out reflect its attitudes toward the public.

The impression a letter creates depends upon both its appearance and its tone. A letter which shows erasures and pen written corrections gives an impression that the sending agency is slovenly. Similarly, a rude or impersonal letter creates the impression that the agency is insensitive or unfeeling. In preparing letters, the employee should apply principles of style and tone which will serve to create the most favorable impression.

Select the Letter Type. The two most common types of business letters are letters of inquiry and letters of response - that is, "asking" letters and "answering" letters. Whichever type of letter the employee is asked to write, the following guidelines will simplify the task and help to achieve a style and tone which will create a favorable impression on the reader.

Select the Right Format. Several styles of letter format are in common use today, including:

- the indented format,
- the block format, and
- the semi-block format.

Modified forms of these are also in use in some offices. The student should become familiar with the formats preferred for usage in his office, and be able to use whichever form the employer requests.

Know the Letter Elements. Every letter includes certain basic elements, such as:

- the letterhead, which identifies the name and address of the sender.
- the date on which the letter was transmitted.
- the inside address, with the name, street, city, and state of the addressee.
- the salutation, greeting the addressee.
- the body, containing the message.
- the complimentary close, the "good-bye" of the business letter.
- the signature, handwritten by the sender.
- the typed signature, the typewritten name and title of the sender.

In addition, several other elements are occasionally found in business letters:

- the *attention line,* directing the letter to the attention of a particular individual or his representative.
- the *subject line,* informing the reader at a glance of the subject of the letter.

- the *enclosure notation,* noting items enclosed with the letter.
- the *copy notation,* listing other persons who receive copies of the letter.
- the *postscript,* an afterthought sometimes (but not normally) added following the last typed line of the letter.

Be *Brief.* Use only the words which help to say what is needed in a clear and straightforward manner. Do not repeat information already known to the reader, or contained elsewhere in the letter. Likewise, do not repeat information contained in the letter being answered. Rather than repeat the content of a previous letter, one can say something like, "Please refer to our letter dated March 5:"

An employee can shorten his letters by using single words that serve the same function as longer phrases. Many commonly used phrases can be replaced by single words. For example,

Phrase	Single word
in order to	to
in reference to in	about
the amount of	for, of
in a number of cases	some
in view of	because
with regard to	about, in

Similarly, avoid the use of adjectives and nouns that are formed from verbs. If the root verbs are used instead, the writing will be more concise and more vivid. For example,

Noun form	Verb form
We made an adjustment on our books	We adjusted our books
We are sorry we cannot make a replacement of	We are sorry we cannot replace
Please make a correction in our order	Please correct our order

Be on the lookout for unnecessary adjectives and adverbs which tend to clutter letters without adding information or improving style. Such unnecessary words tend to distract the reader and make it more difficult for him to grasp the main points. Observe how the superfluous words, italicized in the following example, obscure the meaning: "You may be *very much* disappointed to learn that the *excessively large* demand for our *highly popular recent* publication, 'Your Income Taxes,' has led to an *unexpected* shortage of this *attractive* publication and we *sadly* expect they will not be replenished until *quite* late this year."

Summarizing, then, a *good letter is simple and clear, with short, simple words, sentences, and paragraphs. Related parts of sentences and paragraphs are kept together and placed in an order which makes it easy for the reader to follow the main thoughts.*

Be Natural. Whenever possible, use a human touch. Use names and personal pronouns to let the reader know the letter was written by a person, not an institution. Instead of saying, "It is the policy of this agency to contact its clients once each year to confirm their status," try this: "Our policy, Mr. Jones, is to confirm your status once each year."

Use Concrete Nouns. Avoid using abstract words and generalizations. Use names of objects, places, and persons rather than abstractions.

Use Active verbs. The passive voice gives a motionless, weak tone to most writing. Instead of "The minutes were taken by Mrs. Smith," say, "Mrs. Smith took the minutes." Instead of "The plans were prepared by the banquet committee," say, "The banquet committee prepared the plans."

Use a Natural Tone. Many people tend to become hard, cold, and unnatural the moment they write a letter. *Communicating by letter should have the same natural tone of conversation used in everyday speech.* One way to achieve a natural and personal tone in the majority of letters is through the use of personal pronouns. Instead of saying, "Referring to your letter of March 5, reporting the non-receipt of goods ordered last February 15, please be advised that the goods were shipped as requested," say, "I am sorry to hear that you failed to receive the items you ordered last February 15. We shipped them the same day we received your letter."

Forms

In most businesses and public service agencies, repetitive work is simplified by the use of *forms*. Forms exist for nearly every purpose imaginable: for ordering supplies, preparing invoices, applying for jobs, applying for insurance, paying taxes, recording inventories, and so on. While the forms encountered in different agencies may differ widely, several principles should be applied in completing any form:

*   *Legibility.* Entries on forms should be clear and legible. Print or type wherever possible. When space provided is insufficient, attach a supplementary sheet to the form.

*   *Completeness.* Make an entry in every space provided on the form. If a particular space does not apply to the applicant, enter there the term "N/A" (for "not applicable"). The reader of the completed form will then know that the applicant did not simply overlook that space.

*   *Conciseness.* Forms are intended to elicit a maximum amount of information in the least possible space. When completing a form, it

is usually not necessary to write complete sentences. Provide the necessary information in the least possible words.

- *Accuracy.* Be sure the information provided on the form is accurate. If the entry is a number, such as a social security number or an address, double-check the correctness of the number. Be sure of the spelling of names, No one appreciates receiving a communication in which his name is misspelled.

Memoranda

The written communications passing between offices or departments are usually transmitted in a form known as *"interoffice memorandum."* The headings most often used on such "memos" are:

- TO: identifying the addressee,
- FROM: identifying the sender or the originating office,
- SUBJECT: identifying briefly the subject of the memo,
- DATE: identifying the date the memo was prepared.

Larger agencies may also use headings such as FILE or REFERENCE NO. to aid in filing and retrieving memoranda.

In writing a memo, many of the same rules for letter-writing may be applied. Both the appearance and tone of the memo should create a pleasing impression. The format should be neat and follow the standards set by the originating office. The tone should be friendly, courteous, and considerate. The language should be clear, concise, and complete.

Memos usually dispense with salutations, complimentary closings, and signatures of the writers. In most other respects, however, the memorandum will follow the rules of good letter-writing.

Minutes of Meetings

Most formal public-service organization conduct meetings from time to time at which group decisions are made about agency policies, procedures, and work assignments. The records of such meetings are called *minutes.*

Minutes should be written as clearly and simply as possible, summarizing only the essential facts and decisions made at the meeting. While some issue may have been discussed at great length, only the final decision or resolution made of it should be recorded in the minutes. Information of this sort is usually included:

- Time and place of the call to order,
- Presiding officer and secretary,
- Voting members present (with names, if a small organization),

- Approval and corrections of previous minutes,
- Urgent business,
- Old business,
- New business,
- Time of adjournment,
- Signature of recorder.

Minutes should be written in a factual and objective style. The opinions of the recorder should not be in evidence. Every item of business coming up before a meeting should be included in the minutes, together with its disposition. For example:

- "M/S/P (Moved, seconded, passed) that Mr. Thomas Jones take responsibility for rewriting the personnel procedures manual."
- "Discussion of the summer vacation schedule was tabled until the next meeting."
- "M/S/P, a resolution that no client of the agency should be kept waiting more than 20 minutes for an interview."

Note that considerable discussion may have surrounded each of the above items in the minutes, but that only the topic and its resolution are recorded.

Short Reports

The public-service employee often is called upon to prepare a short report gathering and interpreting information on a single topic. Reports of this kind are sometimes prepared so that all the relevant information may be assembled in one place to aid the organization in making certain decisions. Such reports may be read primarily by the staff of the organization or by others closely related to the decision-making process.

Reports may be prepared at other times for distribution to the public or to other agencies and institutions. These reports may serve the purpose of informing public opinion or persuading others on matters of public policy.

Whatever the purpose of the short report, its physical appearance and style of presentation should be designed to create a favorable impression on the reader. Even if the report is distributed only within the writer's own unit, an attractive, clear, thorough report will reflect the writer's dedication to his assignment and the pride he takes in his work.

Some guidelines which will assist the trainee in preparation of effective short reports include use of the following:

- A good quality paper;
- Wide and even margins, allowing binding room;

- An accepted standard style of typing;
- A title page;
- A table of contents (for more lengthy reports only);
- A graphic numbering or outlining system, if needed for clarity;
- Graphics and photos to clarify meaning when useful;
- Footnotes, used sparingly, and only when they contribute to the report;
- A bibliography of sources, using a standard citation style.

A discussion of the organization of content for informational reports follows later in this document.

News Releases

From time to time, the public-service employees may be called upon to prepare a news release for his agency. Whenever the activities of the agency are newsworthy or of interest to the public, the agency has an obligation to report such activities to the press. The most common means for such reporting is by using the press release. Most newspapers and broadcasting stations are initially informed of agencies' activities by news releases distributed by the agencies themselves. Thus, the news release is a basic tool for communicating with the public served by the agency.

The news release is written in news style, with these basic characteristics:

• Sentences are short and simple.

• Paragraphs are short (one or two sentences) and relate to a single item of information.

• Paragraphs are arranged in *inverted order*—the most important in information appears first.

• The first or *lead* paragraph summarizes the entire story. If the reader went no further, he would have the essential information.

• Subsequent paragraphs provide further details, the most important occurring first.

• Reported information is attributed to sources; that is, the source of the news is reported in the story.

• The expression of the writer's opinions is scrupulously avoided.

• The 5 W's (who, what, why, where, when) are included.

News releases should be typed double spaced on standard 8 1/2 x 11 paper, with generous margins and at least 2" of open space above the lead paragraph. Do not write headlines - that is the editor's job. At the top of the first page of the release include the name of the agency releasing the story and the name and phone number of the person to contact if more information is needed. If the release runs more than one page, end each page with the word "-more-" to indicate that more copy follows. End the release with the symbols "###" to indicate that the copy ends at that point.

Accuracy and physical appearance are essential characteristics of the news release. Typographical errors, or errors of fact, such as misspelled names, lead editors to doubt the reliability of the story. Great care should be taken to assure the accuracy and reliability of a news release.

2. <u>REPORTING ON A TOPIC</u>

At one time or another, most public-service employees will be asked to prepare a report on some topic. Usually the need for the report grows out of some policy decision contemplated by the agency for which full information must be considered. For example:

- Should the agency undertake some new project or service?
- Should working conditions be changed?
- Are new specialists needed on the staff?
- Or should a branch office be opened up?

Or any of a hundred other such decisions which the agency must make from time to time.

When called upon to prepare such a report, the employee should have a model to follow which will guide his collection of information and will help him to prepare an effective and useful report.

As with other forms of written communication, both the physical appearance and content of the report are important to create a favorable impression and to engender confidence. The physical appearance of such reports has been discussed earlier; additional suggestions for reports are given in Unit 3. Basic guidelines follow below for organizing and preparing the content.

Preparation for the Report

What is the Purpose of the Report? The preparer of the report should have clearly in mind <u>why</u> the report is needed:

- What is the decision being contemplated by the agency?
- To what use will the report be put?

Before beginning to prepare the report, the writer should discuss its purpose fully with the decision-making staff to articulate the purpose the report is intended to serve. If the employee is himself initiating the report, it would be well to discuss its purpose with colleagues to assure that its purpose is clear in his own mind.

What Questions Should the Report Answer? Once the purpose of the report is clear, the questions the report must answer may begin to become clear. For example, if the decision faced by the agency is whether or not to offer a new service, questions may be asked such as these:

- What persons would be served by the new service?

- What would the new service cost?
- What new staff would be needed?
- What new equipment and facilities would be needed?
- What alternative ways exist for offering the service?
- How might the new service be administered?

And so on. Unless the purpose of the report is clear, it is difficult to decide what specific questions need to be answered. Once the purpose is clear, these questions can be specified.

Where Can the Relevant Information be Obtained? Once the questions are clear in the writer's mind, he can identify the information he will need to answer them. Information may usually be obtained from two general sources:

- *Relevant documents.* Records, publications, and other reports are often useful in locating the information needed to answer particular questions. These may be in the files of the writer's own agency, in other agencies, or in libraries.

- *Personal contacts.* Persons in a position to know the needed information may be contacted in person, by phone, or by letter. Such contacts are especially important in obtaining firsthand accounts of previous experience.

The Text of the Report

What are the Answers to the Questions? Once the relevant in-formation is in hand, the answers to the questions may be assembled.

- What does the information reveal? This activity amounts to summarizing the information obtained. It often helps to organize this summary around the specific questions asked by the report. For example, if the report asks in one part, "What are the costs of the new service likely to be?" one section of the report should summarize the information gathered to answer this question.

Organizing the Report. The organization of a report into main and sub-sections depends upon the nature of the report. Reports will differ widely in their organization and treatment. In general, however, the report should generally follow the pattern previously discussed. That is, reports which generally include the following subjects in order will be found to be clear in their intent and to communicate effectively:

- *Description of problem or purpose.* Example: "One problem facing our agency is whether or not we should extend our hours of operation to better serve the public. This report is intended to examine the problem and make recommendations."

- *Questions to be answered.* Example: "In examining this problem, answers were sought to the following questions: What persons would be served? What would it cost? What staff would be needed?"

- *Information sources.* Example: "To answer these questions, letters of complaint for the past three years were examined. Interviews with clients were conducted by phone and in person, phone interviews were conducted with the agency directors in Memphis, Philadelphia, and Chicago,"

- *Summary of findings.* Example: "At least 25 percent of the agency's clients would be served better by evening or Saturday service. The costs of operating eight hours of extended service would be negligible, since the service could be provided by rescheduling work assignments. The present staff report they would be inconvenienced by evening and Saturday work assignments."

<u>*The Writer's Responsibilities.*</u> It is the writer's responsibility to address finally the original purpose of the report. Once the questions have been answered, an informed judgment can be made as to the decision facing the agency. It is at this stage that the writer attempts to draw conclusions from the information he has gathered and summarized. For example, if the original purpose of the report was to help make a decision about whether or not the agency should offer a new service, the writer should draw conclusions from the information and recommend either for or against the new service.

<u>*Conclusions and Recommendations,*</u> Example: "It appears that operating during extended hours would better serve a significant number of clients. The writer recommends that the agency offer this new service. The present staff should be given temporary assignments to cover the extended hours. As new staff are hired to replace separating persons, they should be hired specifically to cover the extended hours."

3. ## PERSUASIVE WRITING

Often in life, people are called upon to persuade individuals and groups to adopt ideas believed to be good, or attitudes favorable to ideas thought to be worthwhile or behavior believed to be beneficial. The public service employee may find he must persuade the staff of his own agency, his superiors, the clients of the agency, or the general public in his community.

Persuading others by means of written and other forms of communication is a difficult task and requires much practice. Some principles have emerged from the study of persuasion which may provide some guidelines for developing a model for persuasive writing.

General Guidelines for Writing Persuasively

Know the Credibility of the Source. People are more likely to be persuaded by a message they perceive originates from a trustworthy source. Their trust is enhanced if the source is seen as authoritative, or knowledgeable on the issue discussed in the message. Their trust is increased also if the source appears to have nothing to gain either way, has no vested interest in the final decision. Then, the assertions made in persuasive writing should be backed up by referencing trustworthy and disinterested information sources.

Avoid Overemotional Appeals. Appealing to the common emotions of man—love, hate, tear, sex, etc.—can have a favorable effect on the outcome of a persuasive message. But care should be taken because, if the appeal is too strong, it can lead to a reverse effect. For example, if an agency wanted to persuade the public to get chest X-rays, it would have much greater chance of success if it adopted a positive and helpful attitude rather than trying to frighten them into this action. For instance, appealing mildly to the sense of well-being which accompanies knowledge of one's own good health, instead of shocking the public by showing horror pictures of patients who died from lack of timely X-rays.

Consider the Other Man's Point of View. To persuade another to one's own point of view, should the writer include information and arguments <u>contrary</u> to his own position? Or should he argue <u>only</u> for his own side?

Generally, it depends on where most of the audience stand in the first place. If most of the audience already favor the position being advocated, then the writer will probably do better including only information favorable to his position. However, if the greater part of the audience are likely to oppose this position, then the writer would probably be better off including their arguments also. In this case, he may be helping his cause by rebutting the opposing arguments as he introduces them into the writing.

An example of this technique might occur in arguing for such an idea as a four-day, forty-hour workweek. Thus: "Many people feel that the ten-hour day is too long and that they would arrive home too late for their regular dinner hour. But think! If you have dinner a littler later each night, you'll have a three-day weekend every week. More days free to go fishing, or camping. More days with your wife and children." That is good persuasive writing!

Interpersonal Communications

The important role of interpersonal communication in persuading others—face-to-face and person-to-person communications—has been well documented. Mass mailings or printed messages will likely have less effect than personal letters and conversations between persons already known to each other. In any persuasion campaign the personal touch is very important.

An individual in persuading a large number of persons will likely be more effective if he can organize a letter-writing campaign of persuasive messages written by persons favorable to his position to their friends and acquaintances, than if his campaign is based upon sending out a mass mailing of a printed message.

Conditions for Persuading. In order for an audience of one or many to be persuaded in the manner desired, these conditions must be met:

- the audience must be _exposed_ to the message,
- members of the audience must _perceive_ the intent of the message,
- they must _remember_ the message afterwards,
- each member must _decide_ whether or not to adopt the ideas.

Each member of the audience will respond to a message differently. While every person may receive the message, not everyone will read it. Even among those who read it, not everyone will perceive it in the same way. Some will remember it longer than others. Not everyone will decide to adopt the ideas. These effects are called _selective exposure, selective perception, selective retention,_ and _selective decision._

The Persuasion Campaign. How can one counteract these selective effects in persuading others? One thing that is known is that _people tend to be influenced by persuasive messages which they are already predisposed to accept._ This means a person is more likely to persuade people a little than to persuade them a lot.

In planning a persuasion campaign, therefore, the messages should be tailored to the audiences. Success will be more likely if one starts with people who believe _almost_ as the writer wants to persuade them to believe—people who are most likely to agree with the position advocated.

The writer also wants to use arguments based on values the particular audience already accepts. For example, in advocating a new teen-age job program, he might argue with business men that the program will help business; with parents, that it will build character; with teachers, that it is educational; with taxpayers, that it will reduce future taxes; and so on.

The idea is to find some way to make sure that each member of the particular audiences reached can see an advantage for himself, and for the writer to then tailor the messages for those audiences.

4.   INSTRUCTIONAL WRITING

Another task that the public-service employee may expect to face from time to time is the instruction of some other person in the performance of a task. This may sometimes involve preparing written instructions to other employees in the unit, or preparing a training manual for new employees.

It may sometimes involve preparing instructional manuals for clients of the unit, such as "How to Apply for a Real Estate License," "How to Bathe your Baby," or "How to Recognize the Symptoms of Heart Disease."

Whatever the purpose or the audience, certain principles of instruction may be applied which will help make more effective these instructional or training communications. These are: *advance organizers, practice, errorless learning,* and *feedback.*

Advance Organizers

At or near the beginning of an instructional communication, it helps the learner if he is provided with what can be called an "advance organizer." This element of the communication performs two functions:

- it provides a framework or "map" for the leader to organize the information he will encounter,
- it helps the learner perceive his purpose in learning the tasks which will follow.

The first paragraphs in this section, for example, serve together as an advance organizer. The trainee is informed that he may be called upon to perform these tasks in his job *(perceived purpose),* and that he will be instructed in advance organizers, practice, errorless learning, and feedback *(framework, or "map").*

Practice

The notion of *practice makes perfect* is a sound instructional principle. When trying to teach someone to perform a task by means of written communication, the writer should build in many opportunities for practicing the task, or parts of it. This built-in practice should be both appropriate and active:

- *Appropriate practice* is practice which is directly related to learning the tasks at hand.

- *Active practice* is practice in actually performing the task at hand or parts of it, rather than simply reading about the task, or thinking about it.

By inserting questions into the text of the communication, by giving practice quizzes, exercises, or field work, one can build into his instructional communication the kind of practice necessary for the reader to readily learn the task.

Errorless Learning

The practice given learners should be easy to do. That is, they should not be asked to practice a task if they are likely to make a lot of mistakes. When a mistake is practiced it is likely to recur again and again, like spelling "demons," which have been spelled wrong so often it's difficult to recall the way they should be spelled. Because it is better to practice a task right from the first, it is important that learners do not make errors in practice.

- One method for encouraging correct practice is to give the reader hints, or *prompts,* to help him practice correctly.

- Another method is to instruct him in a logical sequence a little bit at a time. Don't try to teach everything at once. Break the task down into small parts and teach each part of the task in order. Then give the learner practice in each part of the task before giving him practice in the whole thing.

- A third way of encouraging errorless learning is to build in practice and review throughout the communication. The learner may forget part of the task if the teacher doesn't review it with him from time to time.

Remember, people primarily learn from what they <u>do</u>, so build in to the instructional communication many opportunities for the learner to practice correctly all of the parts of the task required for learning, first separately and then all together.

Feedback

The reader, or learner, can't judge how well he is learning the task unless he is informed of it. In a classroom situation, the teacher usually confirms that the learner has been successful, or points out the errors he made, and provides additional instruction. An instructional communication can also help learners in the same way, by providing *feedback* to the learner.

Following practice, the writer should include in his instructional communication information which will let the reader know whether he performed the task correctly. In case he didn't, the writer should also include some further information which will help the reader perform it correctly next time. This feedback, then, performs two functions:

- it helps the learner confirm that his practice was done correctly, and

- it helps him correct his performance of the task in case he made any errors.

Feedback will be most helpful to the learner if it occurs immediately following practice. The learner should be brought to know of his success or his errors just as soon as possible after practice.

STUDENT LEARNING ACTIVITIES

- Write "asking" and "answering" letters, and answer a letter of complaint, using the format assigned by the teacher.

- Write memoranda to other "offices" in a fictitious organization. Plan a field trip using only memos to communicate with other students in the class.

- Take minutes of a small group meeting. Or attend a meeting of the school board and take minutes.

- Write a short report on a public service occupation of special interest to you.

- Write a 15-word telegram reserving a single room at a hotel and asking to be picked up at the airport.

- Write a news release announcing a new service offered to the public by your agency.

- Based upon hearing a reading or pretaping of a report, summarize the report in news style.

- View films on effective communication, for example, *Getting the Facts, Words that Don't Inform,* and *A Message to No One.*

- For a given problem or purpose, compile a list of specific questions you would need to answer to write a report on the topic.

- For a given list of questions, discuss and compile a list of information sources relevant to the questions.

- As a member of a group, consider the problem of "What field trip should the class take to help students learn how to write an effective news release?" What questions will you need to answer? Where will you obtain your information?

- As a member of a group, gather the information and prepare a short report based on it for presentation to the class.

- Write a report on a problem assigned by your teacher.

- Write a brief persuasive letter to a friend on a given topic. Assume he does not already agree with you. Apply principles of source credibility, emotional appeals, and one or both sides of the issue to persuade him.

- Plan a persuasive campaign to persuade a given segment of your community to take some given action.

- Write a short instructional communication on a verbal learning task assigned by your teacher.

- Write a short instructional communication on a learning task which involves the operation of equipment.

- Try your instructional communications with a fellow student to check for errors during practice.

TEACHER MANAGEMENT ACTIVITIES

- Have students practice letter writing. Assign letters of "asking" and "answering." Read them a letter of complaint and ask them to write an answering letter. Establish common rules of format and style for each assignment. Change the rules from time to time to give practice in several styles.

- Have small groups plan an event, such as a field trip, assigning the various tasks to one another using only memoranda. Evaluate the effectiveness of each group's memo writing by the speed and completeness of their planning.

- Have the class attend a public meeting. Assign each the task of taking the minutes. Evaluate the minutes for brevity and completeness.

- Encourage each student to prepare a short report on a public service occupation of special interest to himself.

- Give the students practice in writing 15-word telegrams.

- Have the students prepare a news release announcing some new service offered to the public, such as "Taxpayers can now obtain help from the Internal Revenue Service in completing their income tax forms as a result of a new service now being offered by the agency."

- Give the students practice in summarizing and writing leads by giving them the facts of a news event and asking them to write a one or two-sentence lead summarizing the significant facts of the event.

- Read a speech or a story. Have students write a summary and a report of the speech or story in news style.

- Show films on effective communication, for example, *Getting the Facts, Words that Don't Inform,* and *A Message to No One.*

- State a general problem and have each student prepare a list of the specific questions implied by the problem.

- State a list of specific questions and discuss with the class the sources of information which might bear upon each of the questions.

- Have small groups consider and write short reports jointly on the general problem, "What field trip should the class take to help students learn how to write an effective news release?" Have each group identify the specific questions to be answered, with sources for needed information.

- Have each student identify and prepare a short report on a general problem of interest.

- Assign students to work in groups of three or four to draft a letter to a friend to persuade him to make a contribution to establish a new city art museum.

- Assign the students to groups of five or six, each group to map out a persuasive campaign on a given topic. Some topics are "Give Blood," "Get Chest X-Ray," "Quit Smoking," "Don't Litter," "Inspect Your House Wiring," etc.

- Have each student identify a simple verbal learning task and prepare an instructional communication to teach that task to another student not familiar with the task.

- Have each student prepare an instructional manual designed to train someone to operate some simple piece of equipment, such as an adding machine, a slide projector, a tape recorder, or something of similar complexity.

- Have each student try his instructional communication out on another student, unfamiliar with the task. He should observe the activities and responses of the trial student to identify errors made in practice. He should revise the communication, adding practice, review, and prompts wherever needed to reduce errors in practice.

EVALUATION QUESTIONS

Written Communications

1. Which type of letter would be correct for a public service worker to send?   1.____

   A. A letter containing erasures
   B. A letter reflecting goodwill
   C. A rude letter
   D. An impersonal letter

2. Memos usually leave out: 2.____

   A. Complimentary closings
   B. The name of the sender
   C. The name of the addressee
   D. The date the memo was sent

3. A good business letter would not contain: 3.____

   A. Short, simple words, sentences, and paragraphs
   B. Information contained in the letter being answered
   C. Concrete nouns and active verbs
   D. Orderly placed paragraphs

4. In writing business letters it is important to: 4.____

   A. Use a conversational tone
   B. Use a hard, cold tone
   C. Use abstract words
   D. Use a passive tone

5. Messages between departments in an agency are usually sent by: 5.____

   A. Letter
   B. Memo
   C. Telegram
   D. Long reports

6. Repetitive work can be simplified by the use of: 6.____

   A. Memos
   B. Telegrams
   C. Forms
   D. Reports

7. In filling out forms and applications, it is important to be: 7.____

   A. Legible
   B. Complete
   C. Accurate
   D. All of the above

8. Memos should be:

    A. Clear
    B. Brief
    C. Complete
    D. All of the above

8.____

9. Minutes of meetings should not include:

    A. The opinions of the recorder
    B. The approval of previous minutes
    C. The corrections of previous minutes
    D. The voting members present

9.____

10. Reports are written by public service workers to:

    A. Assemble information in one place
    B. Aid the organization in making decisions
    C. Inform the public and other agencies
    D. All of the above

10.____

11. News releases should include:

    A. A lead paragraph summarizing the story
    B. Long paragraphs about many topics
    C. The writer's opinion
    D. All of the above

11.____

12. Readers of news releases and reports are influenced by the:

    A. Content of the material
    B. Accuracy of the material
    C. Physical appearance of the material
    D. All of the above

12.____

13. The contents of a report should include:

    A. A description of the problem
    B. The questions to be answered
    C. Unimportant information
    D. A summary of findings

13.____

14. People tend to be influenced easier if:

    A. They can see something in the position that would be advantageous to them
    B. They are almost ready to agree anyhow
    C. The appeal to the emotions is not overly strong
    D. All of the above

14.____

———

KEY (CORRECT ANSWERS)

1. B
2. A
3. B
4. A
5. B

6. C
7. D
8. D
9. A
10. D

11. A
12. D
13. C
14. D

WRITING FOR SPEAKING

HOW TO PREPARE AN EFFECTIVE SPEECH OR BRIEFING

The first counsel to be given to any speaker is to determine what he is going to do and then do it—and nothing more.

The question is: how to do it? The answer to that is not as easy as you might suspect, but here are a few tips and suggestions:

The pattern of a speech or script is fairly standardized. Most talks open with an introduction. Next they proceed to develop a theme or subject. Then most speakers end their talks with a summary in the form of a conclusion. A good speaker I know recommends this formula: "First tell your audience what you are going to say, then say it, and close by summarizing what you said."

DEFINE YOUR MAIN POINT

As a start, the simplest procedure is to define your main points in simple declarative statements. The odds are that if your talk cannot be summarized in three or four simple declarative sentences, it should be restructured.

Now that you have defined the elements of your talk, it is time to go to work to develop an outline. Then you should write a first draft.

WRITE THE FIRST DRAFT

Quite frequently you will find that your first draft is entirely too long or too short. One of the hard facts concerning public speaking or briefings is that you are expected to accomplish your objective within a definite time span. Your audience wants its talks done by the clock. This can pose problems. You may find that the harder you work on your talk the more intractable it becomes; it is still either too long or too short. The only remedy for this situation is sweat and more sweat.

Of course if you are really a gifted speaker you don't need to watch the clock. If you aren't, you had best prepare your talk to meet this exact timing.

DEVELOP COHERENCE

One of our greatest failures in speaking is a lack of coherence. We think the audience ought to be able to follow us when we set up a row of apparently unrelated facts. We think the audience ought to discern a design in these unconnected facts. This is exasperating to the audience. It wants to be led coherently from the beginning to the end. For that reason your first job should be to see to it that you have a coherent talk, which proceeds logically from beginning to end.

USE QUOTATIONS IF—

Don't shy away from quotations which help you make a point. Properly used, they can enhance any speech. I would, however, add this caution: Don't quote poetry unless you have a trained voice. Believe it or not, poetry is very difficult to read aloud, and a bungled rendition of a poetic passage can be very embarrassing.

BEWARE OF GOBBLEDYGOOK

Another caution which should be faithfully observed is this: Beware of gobbledygook and "bureaucrateze" in your writing. The esoteric word and office slang may hopelessly confuse other people. Audiences properly resent tortuous verbalisms and obscure locutions.

The dictionary is full of perfectly good, well understood words. Why replace them with hard-to-understand words, or made-up words which only confuse? In other words, stick to plain simple English.

USE VISUAL AIDS IF—

Graphics—slides, vu-graphs, flip charts, blackboards or what have you—are sometimes called visual aids, and they should be *just that*. If, for example, there is no need for a slide, don't use it. There is nothing especially effective about having a slide on the screen every minute you are talking. As a matter of fact a slide can detract from your message at times. A visual aid should clarify or "punch up" a point. If it merely repeats what you are already saying there is no need for it, so why use it?

If graphics help—if they improve—if they enhance your talk above and beyond what you can do with words, use them. But don't use them unless they do. Many Government briefings could be done with fewer graphics and the result would be a better product.

WRITE YOUR TALK OUT

Should you go so far as to write your talk out at full length? In the name of Heaven, do! You may be amazed at how much of your talk reads badly—at first. You may even be inclined to agree that great talks are not written—they are *re*written. Ideas that on the first *writing* seem to be sound may at first *reading* prove to be irrelevant to your subject. I recommend that you write it out and read it several times.

MEMORIZE YOUR SPEECH *IF*—

Now you've written your talk and you are getting ready to present it. Should you memorize it? Here authorities vary. Remember this, if your talk is coherent and proceeds logically through four or five simple declarative statements, you will not need to memorize it. Once you are on your feet, your ideas will flow with the outline—or manuscript—if you have done your homework.

Don't forget this, there are two types of speakers who read talks. The first of these is the speaker who is afraid of being misquoted. Hence, he usually reads his manuscripts verbatim. The other type reads his speech because he hasn't prepared it well enough to follow the outline or manuscript without reading every single word. As a general rule, it is better to appear to read only the parts of a speech that are in quotes.

PRACTICE DELIVERING IT

Whether or not you plan to read your talk, you ought to practice *delivering* it. You would be surprised at the number of traps and pitfalls there are if you plunge ahead without adequate preparation of the presentation. Too many people read their manuscripts to themselves several times and feel that they have made an adequate effort to be ready to deliver it. This is good but you can do better.

It is a good idea, in fact, to practice delivering the speech just as you will give it before the audience—stand up and deliver your talk aloud. This will let you get used to the sound of your voice and it will help you master hard-to-say words. It may even keep you from mumbling and spoiling your flights of eloquence.

Learning by doing can't be surpassed. Most accomplished performers have learned by rehearsing their talk exactly as they planned to present it to their audience. Why speakers forget this is not clear, yet often a speaker with a well-prepared talk makes a very faulty delivery because the words sound strange to him even though they don't *look* strange.

Finally, perhaps the best prescription for a good talk or briefing is this: rewrite and rewrite, rehearse and rehearse.

WRITING THE SPEECH IS ONLY THE BEGINNING!

Overly simplified statements such as "he died of heart failure" or "the car stopped because of engine trouble" may be all right for general public consumption. But the doctor and the mechanic face the much more involved job of specifically diagnosing the trouble.

Equally oversimplified is the request "write a speech for the general." For the speech writer must do much more than simply pound out words on his typewriter.

First, of course, there are the obvious jobs of acquiring input from technical specialists, if such is required, and of outlining a cohesive presentation.

STUDY THE SPEAKER

Then, the writer should, if possible, get to know the speaker well enough to understand his speech style and characteristics—does he use short, simple words and sentences in staccato style or does he tend to use more elaborate words and sentence structure? Does he like to inject humor and, if so, does he do it well? What words and sentence structure must be avoided because he has difficulty with them?

STUDY THE AUDIENCE

But there are other elements to the professionally produced speech that sometimes are overlooked. For example, what is the audience he will address? Is it technical, scientific, professional, or general public—or a mixture of types? The answer to these questions will determine the type of language appropriate for the presentation.

There also are other questions to be answered before a line is written. For example, what are the special interests or concerns of the groups to be addressed?

OTHER THINGS TO CONSIDER

Here are some other points to consider: Should the language be technical or man-in-the-street? Serious or humorous? Detailed or "broad brush"? Should the speech be long or short? Are illustrations appropriate? If so what kind? Would supplemental handout materials be valuable—outline, highlights, charts, statistics, additional factual material?

The handout often serves a valuable purpose. It gives members of the audience pieces of paper to refer back to later, so they can refresh their memories, check statistics, etc.

(*Caution:* If handouts are to be used they should never be distributed in advance. You don't want the audience studying pieces of paper rather than concentrating on the speaker. The speaker should announce that they will be distributed, but not until the audience departs.)

Also consider the auditorium characteristics. Is it large or small? Is it equipped with public address system, projector, and screen if they are needed? Can the lights be dimmed or shades pulled?

OTHER SERVICES MAY BE REQUIRED

In addition to the above, the writer may also be expected to:

1. Prepare a fact sheet for the speaker with the above information on the audience and the auditorium characteristics; trip details (who will meet him, where, when); whether a meal will be served; names of program officials and special guests.
2. With the above in mind, prepare a proposed speech outline, recommending for or against visuals and handouts as indicated. (If handouts are suggested, be sure the program director can arrange for their distribution to the departing audience *after* the speech is delivered.)
3. Offer to prepare introductory remarks for the program chairman, also suggested news releases for use before and after speech.
4. Find out if the program chairman wants advance copies of speech and handouts, if any.
5. If possible, arrange to arrive before the speaker to check out mechanics—public address system, projector, screen, lights, ushers, etc. (This can sometimes be done during the reception period when the speaker is meeting program officials and special guests.)

BUSINESS WRITING

Summary:
This handout provides overviews and examples of how to use tone in business writing. This includes considering the audience and purpose for writing.

What is Tone?
"Tone in writing refers to the writer's attitude toward the reader and the subject of the message. The overall tone of a written message affects the reader just as one's tone of voice affects the listener in everyday exchanges"
Business writers should consider the tone of their message, whether they are writing a memo, letter, report, or any type of business document. Tone is present in all communication activities. Ultimately, the tone of a message is a reflection of the writer and it does affect how the reader will perceive the message.

How can I make sure my messages have the appropriate tone?
The writer should consider several things when preparing to write. The following questions will help you to determine the appropriate tone for your message.
- Why am I writing this document?
- Who am I writing to and what do I want them to understand?
- What kind of tone should I use?

Why am I writing this document?
You should take time to consider the purpose of your document in order to determine how you should express the message you wish to convey. Obviously, you want the message to reach your audience, and you will probably want the reader to take some action in response to your message.
When you consider the message and how you wish to express it, the tone of your message will become apparent.

For example:
Suzy is writing a job acceptance letter to an employer but is unsure of the tone she should take in the message. She has decided to accept the position. When she asks herself, "What is my intent upon writing?" she answers, "I want to accept the position, thank the company for the offer, and establish goodwill with my new co-workers." As she writes the letter she quickly assumes a tone that is appreciative for the offer and enthusiastic about beginning a new job.

Who am I writing to and what do I want them to understand?
Who is your audience? Whether it is an employer or a fellow worker, it is essential that you consider your reader before writing any document. Your message will be much more effective if you tailor the document to reach your specific audience. The message you wish to express must be written in a way that will effectively reach the reader.
The tone that you use to write the document directly affects how the reader will interpret what is said.

For example:
Bob is writing a cover letter for a position as a Sales Representative for a newspaper. He is unsure that he will be able to succeed at such a position, and uses phrases such as: "I hope that you will contact me..." "I know that my qualifications are not very impressive, but..."

The reader is likely to interpret these phrases to mean that Bob isn't really qualified for the position or that he doesn't really want the position.

Clearly, Bob is not assuming an appropriate tone. He must consider that:

- He is applying for a position as a Sales Representative.
- He wants the employer to ask him to come in for an interview.
- The employer will look for highly motivated and confident individuals.

If Bob were to consider these things he may rewrite his cover letter to include such phrases as: "You can reach me at 555-2233; I look forward to hearing from you." "My qualifications make me an excellent applicant for this position..."

The tone of the message has changed drastically to sound more confident and self-assured.

What kind of tone should I use?

Fortunately, you can use the same kind of tone for most business messages. "The business writer should strive for an overall tone that is confident, courteous, and sincere; that uses emphasis and subordination appropriately; that contains nondiscriminatory language; that stresses the "you" attitude; and that is written at an appropriate level of difficulty". The only major exceptions to these guidelines are when you need to write a negative business message, such as when you deny a job offer or a customer request.

Here are some general guidelines to keep in mind when considering what kind of tone to use in your letters and how to present information in that tone:

- Be confident.
- Be courteous and sincere.
- Use appropriate emphasis and subordination.
- Use non-discriminatory language.
- Stress the benefits for the reader.
- Write at an appropriate level of difficulty.

Be Confident

You can feel confident if you have carefully prepared and are knowledgeable about the material you wish to express. The manner in which you write should assume a confident tone as well. As you prepare business documents, you want the reader to do as you ask or to accept your decision. In order to make the document effective, you must write confidently.

Consequently, a confident tone will have a persuasive effect on your audience. The reader will become more inclined to accept your position, and will notice the confidence that you have. Employers are inclined to hire individuals that appear confident and sure of their abilities.

This does not mean however; that you should appear overconfident. This can easily be interpreted as arrogant or presumptuous.

For example:

Not: You must agree that I am qualified for the position.

But: My qualifications in the areas of accounting and customer service meet your job requirements.

Be Courteous and Sincere

A writer builds goodwill for him or herself by using a tone that is polite and sincere. It is important to strive for sincerity in tone because without sincerity, politeness can sound condescending

Consider the words and phrases you use in your document and how your reader will likely receive them. If you are respectful and honest, readers will be more willing to accept your message, even if it is negative.

For example:

Not: You didn't read the instructions carefully, thus your system has shut down.

But: The system may automatically shut down if any installation errors occur.

Use Appropriate Emphasis and Subordination

You can help your readers to understand which of your ideas you consider most important by using emphasis and subordination. You can choose from a variety of strategies to emphasize an idea or to subordinate it.

To emphasize an idea, place it in a short sentence. A short and simple sentence will most effectively convey an important idea. You can provide further explanation, sufficient examples, or evidence in following sentences. To subordinate an idea, place it in a compound sentence.

Emphasis: Smoking will no longer be permitted in the building. The committee on employee health and safety reached this decision after considering evidence from researchers and physicians on the dangers of second-hand smoke.

Subordination: The committee on employee health and safety has finished considering evidence, and they have reached the decision that smoking will no longer be permitted in the building. Ideas placed in the first paragraph of a document or message receives the most emphasis, followed by information placed in the last paragraph. You can subordinate an idea by placing it in middle paragraphs of your message because these paragraphs receive the least emphasis.

Use active voice to emphasize the person or thing performing an action and passive voice to emphasize the action that is being performed.

Active: Scientists have conducted experiments to test the hypothesis.

Passive: Experiments have been conducted to test the hypothesis.

Note: In most nonscientific writing situations, active voice is preferable to passive for the majority of your sentences. Even in scientific writing, overuse of passive voice or use of passive voice in long and complicated sentences can cause readers to lose interest or to become confused. Sentences in active voice are generally—though not always— clearer and more direct than those in passive voice. You can recognize passive-voice expressions because the verb phrase will always include a form of be, such as am, is, was, were, are, or been. The presence of a be-verb, however, does not necessarily mean that the sentence is in passive voice. Another way to recognize passive-voice sentences is that they may include a "by the..." phrase after the verb; the agent performing the action, if named, is the object of the preposition in this phrase.

You can also emphasize and subordinate information by letting readers know how you feel about the information.

The amount of space that you devote to an idea will help convey the idea's importance to the reader. Discuss ideas that you want to emphasize in more detail than you do ideas that you want to subordinate.

The language you use to describe your ideas can also suggest how important that idea is. Use phrases such as "most important," "major," or "primary" when discussing ideas you want to emphasize and phrases such as "a minor point to consider" or "least important" to discuss ideas you want to subordinate.

Emphasis: Our primary consideration must be cost.

Subordination: A minor point to consider is appearance
Repeating important ideas is good way to emphasize them as well. Be careful not to overuse this strategy; you will lose your readers' interest if they believe you are needlessly repeating information.
Our primary consideration must be cost - cost to purchase, cost to operate, and cost to maintain.
Any information that stands out from the rest of the text will be emphasized.

Bolding, underlining, CAPITALIZING, indenting, and highlighting will convey emphasis to your reader. Do not use this strategy frequently or the design effect will be lost.

Use Nondiscriminatory Language
Nondiscriminatory language is language that treats all people equally. It does not use any discriminatory words, remarks, or ideas. It is very important that the business writer communicate in a way that expresses equality and respect for all individuals. Discriminatory language can come between your message and your reader. Make sure your writing is free of sexist language and free of bias based on such factors as race, ethnicity, religion, age, sexual orientation, and disability.

- Use neutral job titles
  Not: Chairman
  But: Chairperson
- Avoid demeaning or stereotypical terms
  Not: After the girls in the office receive an order; our office fills it within 24 hours.
  But: When orders are received from the office, they are filled within 24 hours.
- Avoid words and phrases that unnecessarily imply gender.
  Not: Executives and their wives
  But: Executives and their spouses
- Omit information about group membership.
  Not: Connie Green performed the job well for her age.
  But: Connie Green performed the job well.
- If you do not know a reader's gender, use a nonsexist salutation.
  Not: Dear Gentlemen:
  But: To Whom it May Concern:
- do not use masculine pronouns.
  Not: Each student must provide his own lab jacket.
  But: Students must provide their own lab jackets. Each student must provide his or her own lab jacket.

Stress the Benefits for the Reader
Write from the reader's perspective. Instead of simply writing from the perspective of what the reader can do for you, write in a way that shows what you can do for the reader. A reader will often read a document wondering "What's in it for me?" It is your job to tailor your document accordingly.
Not: I am processing your order tomorrow.
But: Your order will be available in two weeks.
Stressing reader benefits will help you to avoid sounding self-centered and uninterested.

Write at an Appropriate Level of Difficulty

It is essential that you write at an appropriate level of difficulty in order to clearly convey your message. Consider your audience and prepare your writing so that the reader will clearly understand what it is that you are saying. In other words, prepare your style of reading to match the reading abilities of your audience. Do not use complex passages or terms that the reader will not understand. Accordingly, do not use simple terms or insufficient examples if the reader is capable of understanding your writing. A competent writer will match the needs and abilities of their reader and find the most effective way to communicate with a particular reader.

What kind of tone should I use with a negative message?

It is especially important to consider tone when you are writing a negative message. In a negative message, such as a document that rejects a job offer or denies a request, be sure to assume a tone that is gracious and sincere. Thank the reader for their input or involvement and carefully state that you cannot comply with their wishes. Follow this response with an explanation as necessary.

It is best not to draw attention to the person performing the action that will likely displease the reader. Therefore, you may want to avoid using active voice when delivering negative messages. You might also avoid stressing the reader benefits unless there are clear benefits to the negative message. It can sound insincere to stress reader benefits in a negative message.

Not: Thank you for offering me the position as General Manager at Simon's Inc. Unfortunately, I am unable to accept the position. I did not think that the position you offered me would utilize my communication and customer-service skills to the degree that I wanted. Therefore, I have accepted a position as Assistant Director at a different company

But: Thank you for offering me the position as General Manager at Simon's Inc. I appreciate your prompt and generous offer. Unfortunately, I am unable to accept the position. I have accepted a different position that will allow me to utilize my communication and customer-service skills.

In some negative messages, you may need to address faults or issues concerning an individual. When writing messages such as this, maintain a professional tone that does not attack the individual but that makes your position on the issue clear.

For example:

Not: I do not understand why you made such discriminatory remarks.
But: Discriminatory remarks are not tolerated in this organization.